Matt Parvin

Matt is a playwright and screenwriter. He trained as part of the Arcola Theatre Writer's Programme in 2015. His theatre credits include *The Noble Nine, Two Roads* (VAULT Festival); *Jam* (Finborough Theatre); *Cousins* (Soho Theatre); *Alice in Wonderland* (Arcola Theatre). He was the recipient of the Oxford New Writing Festival 2013 Best Script Prize, was shortlisted for the Marlowe Society's Other Prize 2018 and has been twice longlisted for the Bruntwood Prize.

First published in the UK in 2020 by Aurora Metro Publications Ltd.
67 Grove Avenue, Twickenham, TW1 4HX
www.aurorametro.com   info@aurorametro.com

Gentlemen and introduction copyright © 2020 Matt Parvin
Cover image courtesy of © 2020 Mihaela Bodlovic
Production: Peter Fullagar
With many thanks to: Marina Tuffier, Didem Uzum, Bella Taylor

All rights are strictly reserved.

For rights enquiries including performing rights, please contact the publisher: rights@aurorametro.com

No part of this publication may be reproduced, stored in or introduced into a retrieval system, or transmitted in any form, or by any means (electronic, mechanical, photocopying, recording or otherwise) without the prior permission of the publisher. Any person who does any unauthorised act in relation to this publication may be liable to criminal prosecution and civil claims for damages.

This paperback is sold subject to the condition that it shall not, by way of trade or otherwise, be lent, resold, hired out, or otherwise circulated without the publisher's prior consent in any form of binding or cover other than that in which it is published and without a similar condition being imposed on the subsequent purchaser.

Printed in the UK by 4edge Printers, Essex.
ISBNs:
(print) 978-1-912430-53-6
(ebook) 978-1-912430-54-3

GENTLEMEN

by

Matt Parvin

AURORA METRO BOOKS

Author's Thanks

This play would not exist if it weren't for some very supportive collaborators, friends and colleagues.

First up: Will Merrick and Tom York. Will and Tom are not only brilliant actors, but super smart dramaturgs too. They provided copious amounts of time and energy in workshops and readings, along with space in their homes, and love for the play. The fact that they were even remotely interested in it kept me working, and there's no way it would be going on now if they hadn't supported it.

Thanks also to: Sami Ibrahim, Charlie Hooper, Tim Drummond, Charlie Metcalfe and Anna Ssemuyaba, Billy Coughlin and Ed Howells, Caitlin Bevan, David Mercatali, Alice Hamilton, Polina Kalinina and Josh Cockroft, Toby Vaughan, Rachel Wilkie, Sebastian Von Massow, Katie Battcock, Tommo Fowler, Anthony Lau and Andy Twyman. Finally: thanks to Richard, Leyla, and the rest of the team at the Arcola for helping to further develop the script, for staging it, and generally for having faith in the play.

CONTENTS

About the Company 6
Cast & Creatives 7
Biographies 8
Introduction 13
The Play: *Gentlemen* 15

About the Company

Arcola Theatre was founded by Mehmet Ergen and Leyla Nazli in September 2000. Originally located in a former textile factory on Arcola Street in Dalston, in January 2011 the theatre moved to its current location in a former paint-manufacturing workshop on Ashwin Street. Arcola has won awards including the UK Theatre Award for Promotion of Diversity, The Stage Award for Sustainability and the Peter Brook Empty Space Award.

Arcola Theatre produces daring, high-quality theatre in the heart of East London and beyond. We commission and premiere exciting, original works alongside rare gems of world drama and bold new productions of classics. Our socially-engaged, international programme champions diversity, challenges the status quo, and attracts over 65,000 people to our building each year. Ticket prices are some of the most affordable in London, and our long-running Pay What You Can scheme ensures there is no financial barrier to accessing the theatre. Every year, we offer 26 weeks of free rehearsal space to BAME and refugee artists; our Grimeborn Festival opens up opera with contemporary stagings at affordable prices and our Participation department creates over 13,500 creative opportunities for the people of Hackney and beyond. Our pioneering environmental initiatives are award-winning, and aim to make Arcola the world's first carbon-neutral theatre.

Gentlemen

Cast and Creatives

Timby	Danny Kirrane
Greg	Will Merrick
Kasper	Ralph Prosser
Director	Richard Speir
Designer	Cecilia Trono
Lighting Designer	Geoff Hense
Sound Designer	Beth Duke
Voice and Dialect Coach	Danièle Lydon
Fight Director	Keith Wallis
Assistant Director	Lucy Waterhouse
Production Manager	Dan Gosselin
Stage Manager	Millie Cousins

Biographies

Danny Kirrane - Timby

Danny's theatre credits include *Vassa*, *The Hunt* (Almeida Theatre); *We're Staying Right Here* (Park Theatre); *As You Like It* (Regent's Park Open Air Theatre); *A Little Hotel On The Side* (Theatre Royal Bath); *Three Sisters* (Young Vic); *Boys, Romeo and Juliet* (Headlong); *Jerusalem* (Royal Court, Apollo Theatre & Broadway); *Tarantula in Petrol Blue* (Aldeburgh Music); *The History Boys* (National Theatre & West End). His television credits include *Don't Forget The Driver*, *Poldark*, *New Blood*, *Hustle*, *Casualty*, *Doctors*, *Young, Unemployed and Lazy*, *The Site* (BBC); *Britannia*, *Critical*, *Trollied* (Sky); *Game of Thrones* (HBO); *Wasted*, *Utopia*, *The Inbetweeners*, *Skins* (Channel 4); *Doctor Thorne*, *Trinity* (ITV); *I Shouldn't Be Alive: Ocean Disaster* (Discovery Channel). His film credits include *Ravers*, *Peterloo*, *Game Over*, *Pirates of the Caribbean: Dead Men Tell No Tales*, *The Hatching*, *Walking on Sunshine*, *Automata*.

Will Merrick - Greg

Will's theatre credits include *Death of a Salesman*, *The Ghost Train* (Manchester Royal Exchange); *All's Well That Ends Well* (Shakespeare's Globe); *The Libertine* (Theatre Royal Haymarket); *Merlin* (Royal & Derngate); *Wendy and Peter Pan* (RSC); *Boys* (Arcola Theatre). His television credits include *Poldark*, *Fail*, *The Rack Pack*, *Count Arthur Strong*, *Atlantis*, *Doctor Who*, *In With The Flynns* (BBC); *Dead Pixels*, *Coming Up: Burger Van Champion*, *Skins* (Channel 4); *Brief Encounters* (ITV). His film credits include *Modern Life is Rubbish*, *7.2*, *About Time*.

BIOGRAPHIES

Ralph Prosser - Kasper

Ralph's tv credits include the upcoming *Alex Rider* (Sony). His film credits include *Where Is Anne Frank?*, *How To Build A Girl*. *Gentlemen* is his professional theatre debut.

Richard Speir - Director

Richard is a director working on new plays, classics and opera. His theatre credits as a director include *Spun* (Arcola Theatre); *Moments* (Hen and Chickens); *Stevie* (SLAM); *DEADLOCK*, *The Nine O'Clock Service* (Theatre503); *Play 2*, *Breakneck* (Old Red Lion), *The Inevitable Disappearance of Edward J. Neverwhere* (STAR). As Assistant Director, his theatre credits include *Witness For The Prosecution* (London County Hall); *Kenny Morgan*, *New Nigerians*, *Gariné* (Arcola Theatre).

Cecilia Trono - Designer

Cecilia is a French performance designer based in London. Her theatre credits as Designer include *The Paradise Circus* (Playground Theatre); *The Blue Hour of Natalie Barney* (Arcola Theatre); *Mites* (Tristan Bates Theatre); *The Ice Cream Boys*, *The Last Ones* (Jermyn Street Theatre). Her theatre credits as Costume Designer include *The Rubenstein Kiss*, *The Curious Case of Benjamin Button* (Southwark Playhouse). Cecilia was nominated for the 2017 Off-West End Award for Best Set Design for her work on *The Last Ones*.

Geoff Hense - Lighting Designer

Geoff is a Lighting Designer and Head of Production at Arcola Theatre. His theatre credits include *Hoard*, *Sitting*, *Keith?*, *The Daughter-in-Law*, *Spun* (Arcola Theatre); *Secret Life of Humans* (New Diorama / Edinburgh

Festival Fringe); *Testosterone* (Edinburgh Festival Fringe / International Tour); *64 Squares* (New Diorama / International Tour); *Richard II* (Arcola Theatre / UK Parliament).

Beth Duke - Sound Designer

Beth is a theatre sound designer and composer based in London. Her theatre credits include *Scenes with Girls* (Royal Court); *Instructions for a Teenage Armageddon* (Old Red Lion); *Head of State, Patricia Gets Ready (for a date with the man that used to hit her), Alice, Lovely & Jason, Boots, Split* (VAULT Festival); *One Under* (Graeae & UK tour); *Superstar* (Southwark Playhouse); *Fox* (Edinburgh Festival Fringe); *Together, Not the Same* (Sadler's Wells); *New Views* (National Theatre); *Queen Margaret, 5, 11, Emilia* (Mountview Academy of Theatre Arts); *Great Expectations* (Geffrye Museum); *Silence* (Mercury Theatre & UK tour); *Around the Block* (Etcetera Theatre); *Eros* (White Bear Theatre); *Breathe* (Tristan Bates Theatre); *A Fantastic Bohemian, Lovesick* (Arcola Theatre); *Boxman* (UK Tour); *Little Did I Know* (Bread & Roses Theatre); *The State of Things* (Brockley Jack Studio). As Associate Sound Designer, her theatre credits include *War of the Worlds Immersive Experience* (56 Leadenhall Street); *A Midsummer Night's Dream* (Tobacco Factory); *Goodbear, Do Our Best* (Edinburgh Festival Fringe); *Dust* (NYTW). Her film credits include *Gaixia, Hydrangea*. Beth is resident Sound Designer at the Almeida Theatre.

Danièle Lydon - Voice and Dialect Coach

Danièle is a Voice and Dialect Coach. Her theatre credits include *All My Sons, Mood Music* (The Old Vic); *Jude, Big Fish, Sex With Strangers, Dry Powder, You and*

I (Hampstead Theatre); *Rutherford And Son*, *The Curious Incident of the Dog In The Night-Time*, *Medea*, *The Motherfu**er With The Hat*, *Man And Superman*, *Treasure Island* (National Theatre); *White Teeth*, *Wife* (Kiln Theatre); *Harry Potter and the Cursed Child* (West End / Broadway / Melbourne); *School of Rock*, *The Lieutenant of Inishmore*, *Bat Out of Hell* (West End); *The Twilight Zone* (Almeida Theatre); *Carousel* (ENO). Her television credits include *Baptiste*, *Poldark*, *The Paradise*, *Boy Meets Girl*, *Inspector George Gently*, *An Inspector Calls* (BBC); *Victoria*, *Vera* (ITV); *Dark Angel* (Fox). Her film credits include *Shipbreakers*, *Where is Anne Frank?*, *Mercy*, *Life*, *Rogue One (A Stars War Story)*, *A United Kingdom*, *Werner Herzog: Salt and Fire*.

Keith Wallis - Fight Director

Keith has worked as a professional fight director for theatre, film and opera for the past twelve years. His recent theatre credits include *Vassa* (Almeida Theatre); *Beautiful Thing* (Tobacco Factory / New Vic Theatre / The Dukes); *Dishoom!* (Watford Palace Theatre / Oldham Coliseum); *Jump Out Of Skin* (Pleasance Theatre); *The Albatross 3rd & Main* (Park Theatre); *Orphans* (Southwark Playhouse); *Arcadia* (English Touring Theatre); *The Whipping Man* (Theatre Royal Plymouth). His film credits include *Lady Macbeth*, *The Innocent*.

Lucy Waterhouse - Assistant Director

Lucy is a choreographer and theatre director based in London. Her recent theatre credits include *Schiele* (Royal Academy of Arts / Katzspace / UK tour); *Accrete* (The Edge). As Assistant Director, her theatre credits include *Witness for the Prosecution* (London County Hall); *Rights to Move* (The Station). As Movement Director, her theatre credits include *La Cenerentola* (Peacock Theatre); *Things We Do Not Know* (Curve Theatre Leicester).

Dan Gosselin - Production Manager

Dan Gosselin is a Production Manager. His recent theatre credits include *seeds* (UK Tour); *Cinderella: A Drag Panto, The Greatest Play in the History of the World...* (Trafalgar Studios); *Dirty Crusty* (Yard Theatre); *Disney in the West-End Summer Pop-Up* (Covent Garden); *Queen of the Mist* (Brockley Jack Studio / Charing Cross Theatre); *Sh!tfaced Showtime* (Underbelly Festival Southbank); *Summer Rolls* (Park Theatre / Bristol Old Vic). Dan has worked as Festival Production Manager for the Durham Drama Festival and Durham Festival of the Arts and as Deputy Head of Lighting for The Warren in Brighton. Dan is also a director of eStage, a collective of theatre people.

Millie Cousins - Stage Manager

Millie is a Stage Manager based in London. Her theatre credits include *Jack and the Beanstalk* (Harlow Playhouse); *Stiletto Beach* (Queen's Theatre Hornchurch); *Starved* (The Hope Theatre); *Exceptional Promise* (The Bush Theatre); *Misterman* (New Wimbledon Studio); *Market Boy* (Union Theatre); *Musical Theatre Showcase* (Fortune Theatre); *Peter Pan* (Princes Theatre); *Apocalypse Laow* (Katzspace); *Millennials: Offended* (Pleasance Theatre); *Little by Little* (Etcetera Theatre); *The Wild Duck* (Almeida Theatre); *In The Heights* (Stockwell Playhouse); *Down and Out LIVE* (Stone Nest). Millie has also worked as Stage Manager for the Liberation International Music Festival.

Introduction

Gentlemen's origins lie in a very old play of mine – one I wrote whilst I was an undergraduate. As is the case with many British undergraduates, I was a naive, arrogant doofus who felt like an emperor because he'd done well at his A-Levels. I started playwriting in my first year, quite enjoyed it, and discovered that one of the many wonderful things about the university was that there were many opportunities for students to stage their writing, regardless of quality or interest. It was fun, and cheap. The third play I wrote was a short piece set in a series of 'welfare meetings'. It was based on some of my own experiences, and some of my own insecurities – including my fear that I was an imposter, and my anger at elements of the behavior of some of my fellow students. Anecdotes from friends about life at the university also fed in.

My key interests were the university's 'welfare system'; and how young men at the university expressed their 'masculinity'. I felt that the former was often flawed, and the latter was often annoying. I felt like – and still feel like – people who insist on their right to say words that don't matter to them, but that cause great pain to others, need to greatly reassess their personal ethics.

I wrote the play, in part, to express these feelings. But, of course, the scenario and the characters I invented asked their own questions, and challenged my feelings on these issues. That was fun, but what was most fun was staging the play in the university, with some brilliant fellow students, for an audience that included some who exemplified or perpetuated these issues. Did these audience members recognize that? Probably not. But I enjoyed it!

A couple of years later I was living in London, and I saw that the actor and sometime director Will Merrick had put out a call for plays from a company he was a part of – No Prophet Theatre. I submitted my play. The company could not stage it, but Will loved it, so we met for brunch in Victoria Park, like everyone else in East London. We decided to try to get the play on, with Will playing the part of Greg. However, as I was discovering at that time, it's hard to get plays on. So years went by.

In that time, I developed the play with Will's help, in various workshops and readings. Most notably, we did a reading in Studio 2 at the Arcola. I had recently been a Production Intern at the theatre, and was soon to be in the Writers Group there, both of which made me love the place – especially their studio spaces, with their beautiful exposed brick walls. In the reading, an actor called Tom York played the part of Kasper, and afterwards Tom took on a similar role to Will – reading new versions of the script, offering ideas, and providing his garden as a space for further readings.

About six months after the Arcola reading, I went to stay in Hamburg with a friend from university. He's extremely generous, so he gave me his room for free, and in that month I completely reworked the play, into *Gentlemen*. It was important, I felt, to make a new play that could speak to a wider audience than the original, and that had broader concerns. As such, the play grew larger, and its focus and questions shifted. I don't think the text was ever specifically set at my old university, but I also reworked it so that the play could be set at a couple of universities. I felt like it could be speaking about any of them, or all of them.

A few more years went by. The Arcola agreed to read the new version and, much to our surprise, decided to put it on. I worked with Richard Speir to get the play into shape, and that's the one you've bought. Compared to the play I wrote whilst an undergraduate, *Gentlemen* is bigger in scope and bears the influence of the collaborators along the way, but its basic concept remains the same. This concept has, to my mind, unfortunately retained its relevance.

Matt Parvin

GENTLEMEN

Matt Parvin

To my uni friends

The play was first performed at the Arcola Theatre, London on 18th March, 2020. Directed by Richard Speir.

Characters:

GREG An English and History undergraduate in his first term at university. 18. His accent is not RP.

KASPER A History undergraduate in his first term at university. 18. Raised with an RP accent.

TIMBY Welfare Officer at a college at the university. Older (26 – 36).

Notes:

Staging: If you need an interval, put it before the Interlude.

Punctuation: When the text is capitalised, it suggests the volume of the character's speech.

/ indicates the line's interruption by the following line of dialogue or action at this point.

– indicates a character being interrupted or interrupting themselves.

... may suggest that the words are trailing off, or that the character is struggling for words.

An 'Ahah' may be a laugh, a snort, or an 'oh, yes'.

Italicised words in lines of dialogue are to be stressed.

Disclaimers: *This text went to press before the end of rehearsals and so may differ slightly from the play as performed. All characters appearing in this work are fictitious.*

ACT ONE

Scene 1

A study in a college at a prestigious British university. Mid-morning, early November.

The study is sort of an office, sort of a lounge. It is very old and fairly messy. Plants, books, biscuit tins and knick-knacks tumble about in complex patterns; chairs of various comfort-levels, coffee and side tables, cupboards, mirrors, shelves, a bin, a desk – though used – sit at resistant angles; pens roll off shelves suddenly. The cleanest things are a record player, a bike, a landline phone and answering machine, and a laptop. If it weren't for the technology, you would think it was the near past. In the darker recesses, the corners of gothic furnishings peek out.

The study is part of a set of rooms that form a kind of flat. Beyond the door to enter is a small hallway, with two doors off – one to a bedroom, and one to a bathroom. The window looks down onto a college quadrangle.

The atmosphere is that of a room perennially waiting for lunch. Autumn light rolls through dirty windows, lying across the scratched, second-hand furniture or lounging with the dust motes. But you can feel the cold from the outer old limestone walls.

Greg stands, in old trainers and college sports stash – hoody and tracky bottoms – speaking quickly. Timby sits in a comfy chair, in a tweed jacket, shirt, and chinos, papers on his lap, fiddling with glasses and looking up at Greg. Kasper sits nearby, at an odd angle, watching them, in an open zip-up hoody, t-shirt and chinos.

GREG You slight me, Sir.

TIMBY Ahah, no, I am not 'slighting' you, Greg. I have, of course, asked you here about the allegations –

GREG Dirty lies, Sir.

TIMBY Well. For the moment, let's just call them –

GREG The murder of my good name.

Slight pause.

TIMBY Ahah, very good. Ye... roguish... No I'm sure Kasper will agree, in fact, that we'd like to all remain on good terms with one another. That we don't want things to get –

GREG Unseemly.

TIMBY 'Unseemly'? No, certainly not; things in here never get unseemly; this is – squash and biscuits. Heated, I was going to say. We won't get heated. Which is tough, I know, when such things as your ability are / in question.

GREG Integrity.

TIMBY Alright.

GREG Honour.

TIMBY Well... It is important, yes, but. You may well be quite stressed, but –

GREG I am quite calm, Sir.

TIMBY But you don't need to be, see. One month in – that is the thick of it. You're settling in. Finding a routine. Getting to know new people, growing to love new places – emotional, intellectual, architectural.

Greg looks to Kasper – 'what?'

TIMBY You'll have societies, hustings, parties – all kinds of new experiences – including, if you're lucky, relationships –

GREG 'Relationships'? Like with girls?

TIMBY Um, yes. Or boys.

GREG Boys?

TIMBY Boys. *(slight pause)* Which take up –

GREG Not boys.

KASPER / Can we –

TIMBY Which take up – I was – time – they take up time, relationships – girls and boys. When you should be eating, or sleeping; doing the basic things living entails. And while you may want to work –

GREG Yes.

TIMBY and play –

GREG In moderation.

TIMBY Exactly, no, yes – You must find balance. I'm loath to admit I myself at times do not. And while 'work hard, play hard' may be our mantra, right – they are unstable entities to mix in large amounts.

GREG I'm terrified.

TIMBY Because they may tip either way, Greg – over-work, under-work – there's risk of, of, of – tipping over the line. Knowing this – having seen this – what I am trying to say is, I understand –

GREG The troubles of sexual relationships.

TIMBY No. Not the –

GREG   You don't –?

TIMBY   This place makes people act out.

GREG   Are you suggesting something, Sir?

TIMBY   There are explanations for misconduct that don't stain the student involved.

A pause.

GREG   I thought we were getting on, Sir.

TIMBY   Good, –

GREG   Now I think I should depart, Sir.

TIMBY   No, Greg, for heaven's sake – I am versed in this. I've experienced it from this side of the fence and yours – I did my Bachelors here, my Masters here, now I'm on the PhD and working here – and, while, yes, I am a smidge older – I understand. Yes? *(He pauses)* So, conceding that we find ourselves in odd emotional states –

GREG   I won't, –

TIMBY   ... in this bubble we call home, –

GREG   I'm perfectly sane

TIMBY   ... what must be asked is –

GREG   so why would I do this?

TIMBY   Well... I was going to ask: were external pressures to blame? However, yes, that's also – Why would you–?

GREG   Act in such a way as to jeopardise everything I've worked for? Everything I've slaved in dark libraries for, sacrificed mighty club nights for?

TIMBY Sure. But really I want to get to the bottom –

GREG Of the well.

TIMBY Well–?

GREG Yes – of the well. A well full of miscommunication and mistrust. That dank, complex place where it's difficult to tell who's right or wrong. Part difficult morals, part supposition, part pure shite.

TIMBY Seems a bit much.

GREG I think it is so important to keep our distance here, Sir. Avoid settling, which way danger lies. Without critical distance, Sir, how will you be able to judge –

TIMBY I'm here to talk.

GREG Right, we talk, then you take out your big gavel and you –

TIMBY You've misunderstood. Welfare Officers don't judge, we listen. Then mediate. Your tutor will decide whether to pass this on to the Dean. I'm here to help.

GREG You are in the admin though, right.

TIMBY Technically. But I am a student too. I'm between. I'm fluid.

Greg looks to Kasper and raises his eyebrows.

TIMBY Dr Harper asked me to chat with you, to check what's up, to see if we can't resolve this little disagreement man-to-man.

GREG Mm yeah, but that makes me wary though, Sir. You see so much institutional prejudice and wrongdoing and cover-ups these days, gotta be careful.

TIMBY Now no, I think that's smart. A lot of young men your age forget that institutions can hold grudges too, which is why –

GREG Gotta resist, haven't you.?

TIMBY Um… In what –

GREG Be aware that sometimes we are victims, unaware.

TIMBY Sometimes.

GREG Pawns in games beyond our comprehension, on boards controlled by higher powers – nasty bureaucrats.

TIMBY I wouldn't –

GREG Work to liberate ourselves from these rotating behemoths. Concoct new social contracts. Make new lands in mind and soul.

TIMBY *(stares)* You've been accused of plagiarising an essay, Greg.

GREG And I am taking that very seriously. Let us be precise here – accused, and only that. You've no proof to rest a pint on.

TIMBY Except for the essay itself.

GREG Not unless you mean verification of my rebuttal.

TIMBY I *do not, no*.

GREG You don't know?

TIMBY No I, I do not, no.

GREG Can you give me the evidence, Sir? Allow me a chance to defend myself, Sir? For is that not my human right, Sir?

Timby checks his watch, looks to Kasper. Kasper shrugs, nods.

TIMBY According to Dr Harper, on October third he agreed that Kasper would write on the question of the importance of General Francisco Franco's leadership in the Spanish Civil War. In the same tutorial, you avoided committing to any topic.

GREG Mm, or did we agree I would defer my decision? Let's –

TIMBY The next week Kasper handed in a 'highly original' argument outlining how Franco's daily routine affected his duties as general. Thirty minutes after the deadline, you handed in the same essay –

GREG No.

TIMBY with the argument shifted about, adjectives changed, and sentences shifted syntactically.

GREG So I didn't hand in the same essay.

TIMBY Mostly the same.

GREG No such thing as 'mostly the same'. Every shift makes it completely different.

TIMBY In essence –

GREG Does an essay have an 'essence'?

TIMBY This isn't a matter of semantics. You obtained Kasper's essay feigning interest – there's an email to prove it –

Greg turns to Kasper.

GREG   Did you–?

KASPER   / You –

TIMBY   and – sorry Kasper – your argument being identical, you'd've incurred the wrath –

GREG   'The wrath'...

TIMBY   ... of your tutor anyway since you failed the basic task.

Timby and Kasper corner Greg with their stares.

GREG   It's not 'identical', no.

TIMBY   Oh no?

GREG   No no.

TIMBY   Please explain.

Kasper throws up his arms.

GREG   With pleasure. Our argument relied on soldiers' and advisors' reports of Franco's day-to-day leadership. His character, his tasks. But this level of detail is where my colleague here stopped. Instead of vaguely stating Franco went about his day, I argued – nay, revealed – on the back of extensive research – Franco had crumpets.

TIMBY   Crumpets?

GREG   Crumpets. The arc of Franco's morning changed before our very eyes. El Capitan that itsy bit heavier, travelling slower between duties. The fearsome leader's buttery fingers smudging maps, annoying and confusing his subordinates. Those delicious little *bollos*, in their passage from hand to mouth to arse, disrupt the image of Franco, Kas and I had previously built. Kas, in essence, forgot one thing: dictators have breakfast too.

Now I hear you say 'Greg, you just added the sentence 'also Franco had some crumpets' – which I definitely did – but if you read the essay carefully, stop to consider the ramifications, you'll see I've subtly undermined the traditional image of Franco, thus answering the question in a different fashion.

TIMBY But –

GREG And unlike Kasper's, I kept to the question – I cut some bits from the conclusion about Franco and the gays, which was totally irrelevant.

KASPER / Queerness under Franco was perse –

TIMBY Greg, really, we need to be respectful of –

GREG And were I to have had more time – I'm saving this for my PhD – I would have also argued Franco was a massive pussy.

TIMBY Greg, please, your language is –

GREG Because without the German and Italians' support, he would not have won the war.

TIMBY Excuse me for putting words in your mouth, Kasper – *(Kasper shakes his head)* but this isn't fair on him – he clearly put a lot of effort and heart into that essay –

GREG He read two books from our reading list and struck a flamboyant, contrarian pose – / That's apparently all that's expected here.

KASPER Can we–?

GREG Do you know how hard it is to research Franco's diet?

TIMBY You didn't really though –

GREG Certainly did.

TIMBY You copied –

GREG Corrected.

TIMBY Kasper's essay and added – all you did was –

GREG All I did was answer him. Look at the bottom of the essay, he's credited.

TIMBY Where? *(He presents his printed copy of the essay)*

GREG Riiiiiiiiiiiiiiight there. *(He points)*

TIMBY That's tiny.

GREG But there.

TIMBY Practically invisible.

GREG But there. Undeniably, absolutely there.

Stalemate. Timby and Greg watch each other. Kasper glances between them.

Timby moves out of Greg's stare, into a contemplative stance.

TIMBY Greg, I'll let you in on a little something I've learnt in my time here. College – and, in fact, the university as a whole – is a community.

GREG ... Christ...

TIMBY One we work together to make work.

GREG Work to work.

TIMBY Yes.

GREG To work.

TIMBY Indeed, yes, and if we work, they really work. Just like families work. We're a family. This is how we all function properly – stay above water, so to speak. We are like a, like a –

Do you like sports?

GREG Do I like sports?

TIMBY Yes do you like sports?

GREG Do I like sports.

TIMBY We are like a sports team, aren't we? We pass the balls, care for each other –

GREG Do you like sports?

TIMBY Do I like sports?

GREG Yeah do you like sports?

TIMBY Yes I like sports.

GREG Which sports?

TIMBY Well... cricket.

GREG Favourite team?

TIMBY England.

GREG Player?

TIMBY I'm loath to be partial – I'm speaking of how they cohere –

GREG But –

TIMBY Kasper, do you like sports?

Kasper hesitates.

KASPER / Uh. I like –

GREG *(He snorts)* He wouldn't come to rugby. Odd, as I'd heard he liked to catch balls.

Kasper stares at Greg; Timby notices but speaks over it –

TIMBY They aren't for everyone. Can be quite, aggressive, can't they, sports?

GREG Cricket?

TIMBY Yes. What a game.

What am I saying? What I am saying is you don't undermine your cricket mates, do you? You work with them – lucky to, lucky to –

When you shut this chapter of your life and look back – believe me, you will – saying what the lord happened, that was, that was, an afternoon's light alone – if you can't already feel it at your back – they'll be the people you see. And what you lost by not –

You know you seem incredibly unaware how lucky you are – both of you – *(Kasper and Greg look at each other)*... to be here – at your fingertips, tutors, classmates, a welfare system that –

GREG 'Luck'?

TIMBY Yes, luck.

GREG No luck about it – I worked hard to be here.

TIMBY No, sorry, yes. I simply meant –

GREG This is nonsense, right? All this gay crap –

TIMBY Greg, please, your lang –

GREG 'community', 'welfare' – / it sucks.

KASPER You keep –

GREG   Well it is, it's super gay.

Kasper stares at Greg. He watches Greg very carefully until the end of the scene.

TIMBY   Welfare is crucial to the running of a healthy college.

GREG   You don't wonder whether you might be just inventing problems so / you have something to –

TIMBY   Greg, people come for help daily.

GREG   Sure – you're having an episode, you're spazzing out – come see the Welfare bloke. But in this situation. Kasper's fine. *(Kasper goes to speak)* – I'm fine. Dr Harper is fine – he's told you as a formality – it's one less essay for him to mark. We do two of these a week.

TIMBY   If this were your coursework –

GREG   Isn't though.

TIMBY   You could still face consequences.

GREG   It's fine, I swear.

TIMBY   What if College decides to take away your scholarship? You don't want to risk souring that good faith.

GREG   I don't see why I would have, Sir.

TIMBY   I'd like to go back to your tutor and say –

GREG   Here's what you recount, Sir. Greg gave a robust defense of his innocence. He felt himself to have engaged with a debate popular amongst his cohort. He adores his subject, nay, embodies it. He is the Franco expert; he is the true historian.

Stalemate.

TIMBY Well Greg, I think it's a mistake not to apologise, I / really do.

GREG I value your counsel highly, Sir. But I wouldn't know what I was apologising for.

TIMBY *(He pauses)* If there's nothing else, let's leave it there.

GREG Cheers, Sir.

TIMBY Mm.

Greg gets ready. Kasper does not – as if waiting for Timby to do something more.

TIMBY Timby, please.

GREG If you say so. Cheers, Timby.

Timby puts a smile back on. Greg is ready.

TIMBY What does the rest of the day bring?

GREG Gym, class, long nap, dinner.

TIMBY And the evening?

GREG Wherever the lash takes me.

He grins at Timby, winks at Kasper, and leaves.

A pause. Kasper gets ready, annoyed, watching Timby. Timby's stood thinking.

Timby sees Kasper watching. Timby frowns – 'sorry'.

TIMBY 'The lash'. Sounds rather violent, ahah.

Kasper smiles politely and finishes getting ready.

TIMBY Just drinking, isn't it?

Scene 2

Lunch-time, mid-February.

Timby and Greg sit facing each other. Timby is in a similar outfit, plus a sweater. Greg is in an open zip-up hoody, polo shirt, jeans and old trainers. Between them is a mound of sandwiches, cut into crustless triangles.

Timby clears his throat.

TIMBY How's your day been, Greg?

GREG Ah, you know ... Fried breakfast, bit of reading, STD test.

TIMBY Oh. Are you alright?

GREG Should be. No leaks or anything.

TIMBY Very good. Do you want to, talk about it?

GREG What, the STD test? Do you want me to talk about it?

TIMBY Some your age find it quite distressing.

GREG It wasn't an abortion. An old woman put a plastic blow-dart up my dick.

TIMBY What's that if not distressing?

Greg laughs.

GREG Had a few in your day?

TIMBY Not something I'm keen to go into. *(A short pause)* Well... Let's just say I've had the odd...

GREG Crab?

TIMBY brush.

GREG Thrush?

TIMBY Scare. The odd scare.

A little pause.

GREG Ah, it's all part of the fun, right. You got a lady friend?

TIMBY I don't think it's especially appropriate for me to discuss that. *(Greg stares. A short pause.)* No not right now. I'm between.

GREG Two women? Doff of the old cap, Timby, I didn't know you had it in you.

TIMBY Between partners, I mean.

GREG I see… So it's the Sahara.

TIMBY Sorry?

GREG Death Valley. Eczema. A dry patch… My sympathies.

TIMBY How about you, are you in a relationship?

GREG I'm a Fresher.

TIMBY Right… You're out every night, taking girls on dates.

GREG Dates? Why'd I want to go on dates?

TIMBY Romance… courtship. You're more a wham-bam… wham-bam man.

GREG I wouldn't put it that way, but … I have had enough sex in this last month to kill me. I'm turning it down. Trick is, right, not just to go to every club night there is, but also to be on all the dating apps.

TIMBY Do you not find it a bit, um …

GREG No shame these days, Sir. Here – *(He gets out his phone, unlocks it, passes it over. Timby looks at the open app.)* We should get you on there.

TIMBY Ahah. No. *(He studies it.)* It's very... very well designed, isn't it?

GREG I spend a lot of time curating my online aesthetic. Wanker-speak for making it look nice, sending the odd dick pic. It's like your CV. Except there's no limits on length.

Timby chuckles.

TIMBY Very good. Oh, you've got a 'match'.

GREG Show me. *(Timby does)* Must've been absolutely trashed. Reject her.

TIMBY Just...? *(Greg stares. Timby does so. Greg grins.)* Something now from 'Kara'? Is that Kara Ri –

Greg lurches for the phone.

GREG Give it here. *(Timby hands it over, watches Greg.)* Just a mate. Shags everyone. Hilarious. Massive respect to her. There's actually a club. All the guys that've poked her. Hold meetings. Got a gavel and everything.

TIMBY This club ... I wouldn't like to think –

GREG I'm joking. There's no club.

TIMBY If there is –

GREG Know what, I did get this the other day. *(He pulls from his bag a tattered sheet of paper, and shows one side to Timby. It's a handwritten poem.)* Someone put a poem in my pidge. Think it's from a secret admirer.

TIMBY Old-fashioned.

GREG Right? Maybe there's an untapped market for letter-based flirting.

TIMBY Let's hear it.

GREG You what?

TIMBY I'm dying to know what passes for a love poem these days. Go on. We've got time.

GREG ... okay... *(He stands, slightly confused. As he reads he gets into it.)*
What fool to break the air with chat and grin,
When all around us bursts the afternoon,
And I am loath to be a fool for you,
But then the day will fold and shut so soon.
Oh yes, the day will shut and snarl too soon,
You'll feel it on your collar's verge before
It strokes your nape, whispers your name, and burns.
You'll fall and feel the cobbles of the quad –
Fall and fail to fell the fears that drive you
On to beg me, asking how you came here.
Leaning on your sword, searching cobbles' help,
A thread slips round your neck, burns skin, and breaks.
We fall in love with the afternoon light,
We fall, we fall, we fall, so quick it seems,
Falling endless in the afternoon light.

TIMBY That's... You read it very / well.

GREG No, I mean it's terrible, right.

TIMBY Oh, yes, sure, definitely. Juvenile melancholy. But even such has pleasures, ahah.

GREG Now I hear it, it's kind of angry, right? But... angry sexy?

TIMBY Certainly possible.

Greg sits. You can hear them swallowing.

GREG And how're you, sir?

TIMBY Oh, yes, well. A little washed out. Formal last night – I was on High Table, beside the Master. Another historian.

GREG He's solid, he is.

TIMBY Yes. He had kind words for you, too. Always wonderful to catch up with him. Otherwise. Busy busy. It's that point in the year, you know. Anxiety levels up. In students. All realising how much work they actually have, ahah. Never do, till they do. And... this morning I've been assisting a colleague at another college. You might have heard, actually. One of their first year students took his own life.

GREG Oh... Shitter –

TIMBY Yes, indeed.

GREG No, that was his name.

TIMBY Sorry?

GREG That was his name. Shitter.

TIMBY His name was 'shitter'?

GREG Yeah.

TIMBY His name was Callum.

GREG His nickname, I mean. His nickname: 'Shitter'. 'cause he shat himself. In Freshers Week. On the dance floor at Consortium. Real bad. Just everywhere. They had to close the whole R&B / room –

TIMBY Okay, well –

GREG Then he hangs himself. And shits himself again. 'Shitter' in death as in life, ey.

TIMBY Callum will have a memorial service on / Thursday –

GREG I just think it's ironic. Don't you? He shat himself so he killed himself.

TIMBY Well –

GREG Whereupon he shat himself again. Not the best problem solver, was Shitter. Some just can't hack it, right?

Timby stares. Another pause. Timby goes to his desk. He takes from a drawer some fancy chocolate, gestures with it to Greg; Greg shakes his head. Timby snaps off bits and eats as they talk.

GREG Where is he?

TIMBY Must be busy.

GREG He must be busy? I've got more work than him and I was here on time. God, I'm telling you Timby, I should never have applied for History and English. With English too, I'm … wondering when to sleep. I've been trying to write something for this essay competition, and I'm –

TIMBY What's it on?

GREG Oh, uh. I'm thinking of doing it on like, Schrödinger and Heisenberg? Like, how their theories might've affected narrators, or depictions of observation, in twentieth century novels?

TIMBY That's so interesting.

GREG *(He shrugs)* Tough when you're the hungoverest boy IN THE WORLD.

TIMBY Would you like some squash?

GREG Go on then. *(Timby gets Greg some squash.)* Hey, while we're waiting, you mind if I get changed? *(Timby hesitates)* I've got footy right after is all, gonna be late at this rate.

TIMBY Why not?

A pause while Greg begins to change into his sports gear. Timby sets the squash down before Greg, then moves away.

GREG Cheers mate.

A pause.

TIMBY Especially cold, isn't it?

GREG Yeah, my nips are screaming.

Timby fiddles with various knick-knacks, facing away.

TIMBY What did you, um, get up to last night?

GREG Mate... You know when you've had so many Thin Jimmies you feel the whites of your eyes? Three times this week.

TIMBY Oh my.

GREG By last night I was a husk. Did a TC in the library flowerbeds. Tactical chunder.

TIMBY That was you?

GREG That was my three am pizza Deliveroo. James's rents give him a 'Deliveroo allowance' – mental. Like these guys... They go hard, they're legends, but they're sharp, you know? Last week we replaced every Master's Portrait in Hall with ones of Paxman.

TIMBY I saw those. I thought I was hallucinating.

GREG Good, right.

TIMBY Very good.

GREG That's just what we do.

TIMBY Yes, yes. Yes... I'm not ashamed to admit, that's the kind of thing we used to do when I was here too. Some wild nights.

GREG Like what?

TIMBY Oh, you know... No, it's just a blur now, really. But boozy dinners. Very satirical speeches. After which the, the ruckus, ahah.

GREG Sounds mad.

TIMBY It truly was.

A door opening out in the hall, nearby. Then the door closing.

TIMBY I was speaking to one of the, one of the – to Hugo the other day in the dinner queue. Do you know Hugo?

GREG Which Hugo?

TIMBY Hugo in your year.

GREG In my year? Which Hugo?

TIMBY Big Hugo in your year.

GREG They're both – Tall Hugo or Small Hugo? *(The study door has been opening slowly, and*

Kasper's head appearing.) Small Hugo is taller than Tall Hugo.

TIMBY Smaller than Tall Hugo?

GREG Taller than Tall Hugo; it's ironic. Small Hugo or –

TIMBY Tall Hugo.

GREG Do I know Tall Hugo? Do you know Tall Hugo?

TIMBY Yes, I know Tall Hugo.

GREG In my year – Tall Hugo my room-mate –

TIMBY Yes, Tall Hugo in your year, your room-mate. Suggested I come to Captain's Cocktails. Said you're selling tickets. Could be a laugh, ey.

GREG Ah... No tickets left, mate.

Timby sees Kasper, stands.

TIMBY Yes, hello, Kasper.

GREG Our resident friendly ghost.

TIMBY Come in, come in.

GREG What time d'you call this?

TIMBY Oh it doesn't matter, you haven't missed much.

He sets his hand on Kasper's shoulder, guides him in.

GREG Timby was just telling me about his love life.

TIMBY Not, not really, Greg. Just a chat about... nothing, really. How are you doing, Kas?

GREG	Yeah how's it going, mate, haven't seen you about much.

TIMBY	Let Kas get a word in, Greg. Have a seat, have a sandwich, Kas – make yourself at home. *(Kasper sits. Slight pause.)* After the plagiarism incident –

GREG	Ah – I was cleared of that. Can we strike it from the record?

TIMBY	Sure... Stricken. It's my belief you've received a warning, though.

GREG	Nope.

TIMBY	Okay. Shall we discuss what's been going on, then?

GREG	I'd love to, if I knew what it was. Your email made a few claims, but I haven't the foggiest what it meant. So I'm keen to hear the official line.

TIMBY	No, this is not 'the official line' – this is a chat – to figure out what's been going on before others get involved. But let's be crystal clear with one another. Kasper, and a few other students, have come forward – Are you comfortable with this, Kas? *(Kasper hesitates, nods.)* To say that you've been bullying Kasper for his sexuality.

GREG	Which is? *(Little pause.)* Why don't you outline everything you're accusing me of, in detail, and I'll help you understand the reality.

TIMBY	It is specifically your mocking of his bisexuality.

GREG	Which is?

Little pause.

TIMBY As in ...

GREG I'm fresh to all this stuff, can I get a definition?

Little pause.

TIMBY Bisexuality is ... *(He looks to Kasper. Beat.)* When the person likes both genders.

Beat. Kasper shrugs – 'why are you looking at me?'

GREG Okay, yes, so he's gay.

TIMBY Bi.

GREG Gay.

TIMBY He's bi.

GREG Bi, gay – he's gay.

TIMBY No, / he is –

KASPER I am –

GREG On his way. To gay.

TIMBY No, see, that's a common – Isn't it – that's a miscon –

GREG What's pan?

TIMBY Pan?

GREG Pan, deep pan –

TIMBY Pan is irrelevant.

GREG Ooooooooh, you can't say that.

TIMBY Greg. Help me out here, mate.

GREG Happy to.

Little pause.

TIMBY This is a safe space. Let's remember that. These students cited three incidents.

GREG Pray tell.

TIMBY The first took place in a club –

GREG Which club?

TIMBY Establishment, I believe. *(beat)* Wait, did I get that –

GREG Yeah.

TIMBY 'Establishment'?

GREG Which night, though?

TIMBY A Tuesday.

GREG They all blur – which club night?

Beat.

TIMBY Judges and Sluts.

GREG Of course, Judges and Sluts. Good old Judges and Sluts.

TIMBY During the final song –

GREG *Mr Brightside* – always ends Judges and Sluts.

TIMBY … you took a photo of Kasper stood between a young man and a young woman. The next morning you uploaded it to the…

GREG The what?

TIMBY The… ShagCam.

GREG The what?

TIMBY The ShagCam.

GREG The 'what-Cam'?

TIMBY Shag. Cam.

GREG Oh, the ShagCam.

TIMBY The page where students post pictures ...

GREG Saying who's shagged.

TIMBY Implicating. And your caption was: 'He's going for both. What a greedy boy.' Which impli – Sorry, Kasper, this must be –

KASPER / Please, just –

GREG Was implicating what?

TIMBY That Kasper wanted both the man and – And was making a joke out of the notion.

GREG I don't hear that. I didn't mean that. I know Kas here likes to go to the WonderVan after the club and I have observed he alternates between Doner kebab and a jumbo sausage. I thought the look in his eye – the distant, pensive, yet hungry look in his eye – was suggesting that tonight he'd go for the Doner kebab. And the jumbo sausage.

Timby pauses. Kasper watches Timby.

TIMBY Okay. Incident two. *(Greg snorts. Kasper shakes his head.)* You were in charge of designating characters for the fancy dress bop in third week. You made Kasper, specifically, Elton John.

GREG Yeah, he looks like him.

TIMBY When he protested, you gave him Captain Jack Harkness from *Doctor Who*.

GREG Yeah, he looks like him.

TIMBY How can a man look like both Elton and – The point is both characters are – Well one is gay, the other bisexual.

GREG Really? They're –? That's a coincidence if I ever I –

TIMBY I struggle to believe that.

GREG I'm as shocked as you are.

TIMBY You can see how this looked.

GREG Looked, exactly.

They pause.

TIMBY Incident three: Kasper was helping to get the drinks together for the same bop. When he expressed his distaste at a particular drink, you called him 'massively gay'.

GREG Ah, no, no I didn't, I remember that. I called the drink 'massively gay', because –

TIMBY That is

GREG Because Kasper didn't want to use whiskey in the boptails. Which is massively gay. I mean really, mate, leaving out the whiskey – *(Kasper cringes)* that's so lame –

TIMBY Greg that is offensive.

GREG No, it's not.

TIMBY It offends Kasper and I, therefore...

GREG Just shits and giggles, mate.

TIMBY I don't know what that means.

GREG It's ironic.

TIMBY Regardless. You cannot say these things to other students, you just can't. If you're gay, like Kas –

KASPER / I'm –

GREG But he's not! He's not even –

TIMBY Bi, sorry –

GREG You said –

TIMBY I meant bi.

GREG So how even was me saying 'gay' about him.

TIMBY Ah, but earlier, you thought 'bi' meant 'gay'.

GREG I was joking. Kas is bi. Let's remember that.

A little pause.

TIMBY Look, I know you're stressed with work right now –

GREG That's not –

TIMBY and feel this is wasting your time, but if we have reports from students that –

GREG They're being over-sensitive. It's that time of the month. They need something to plug their holes. In their lives.

Timby pauses. Resets himself.

TIMBY How about, Greg, we come at it from another angle, yes? Let us... assess your relationship with Kasper. Perhaps a bit of role-play.

GREG Love a bit of role-play.

TIMBY Brilliant, great, okay. So you see Kasper in the hallway, let's say, *(Greg nods)* what d'you do? *(Greg pauses)* Go for it. Whatever you do, we're not judging. *(Greg stays paused)* Hey, Greg?

GREG Yeah?

TIMBY You got it? It's what you do, when you see him. *(Greg nods)* You're walking by him, books in hand, got a tute to get to... what do you do? *(Greg moves)* Okay... *(Greg moves towards his squash)* No – *(Greg takes it up and has a sip)* The role-play is what you do when you see him in the hallway. Show me what you do. Show me what you –

Greg grins – Timby pauses.

GREG Yeah? Because, I have no relationship with Kasper. Of any kind. At all.

TIMBY You're in the same college, / same tutorials. You do interact, so –

GREG No but – No but – Beyond that those structures – there's nothing there. Nothing there.

TIMBY Why?

GREG Well we aren't of the same type, you see, / so we don't –

TIMBY Ah, now, see, what does that mean? 'Type'?

GREG Uh... No doesn't mean / anything, really.

TIMBY No, it does, what does it mean?

GREG *(pausing)* We don't move in the same circles. But that's the nature of any social situation, right, people don't always fit in. And those others are rejected. Not always consciously, like. Involuntarily. Not a match.

TIMBY But why, / in this case –

GREG For varying reasons. Maybe they look wrong. Speak wrong. Or just haven't made the effort.

A little pause.

TIMBY In any community –

GREG 'Community', 'community'. Every time you say community, you imagine us gathered round a 'hurth' like a family in Dickens, warming our hands, rosy-cheeked / ragamuffins –

TIMBY No, I'm not thinking of any 'h*a*rths', I assure you. *(He pauses)* I'm –

GREG We aren't round any 'h*u*rths', Timby. I assure you.

TIMBY I know we aren't round the 'h*a*rth'... but –

GREG But that's what you imagine, Sir. You imagine *the 'hurth'*.

TIMBY I do not imagine *the 'harth'* –

GREG You're – I can see it, in your eyes, the flicker of light, *from the 'hurth'*. But you must rid yourself –

TIMBY I –

GREG *of the 'hurth'. Of, the 'hurth'. Rid the 'hurth'. Rid the* –

TIMBY It's –

GREG Have you rid the –

TIMBY I've rid the, the, the – 'hurth', yes – But –

GREG Just because we're in the same environment, confined by the same four walls, doesn't mean we're a community. A community is based on mutual feeling. Mutual, feeling. I have a community: my community. You have a community: your community. Kasper might have a community, I don't –

TIMBY But why –

GREG He's never tried. Really. You've never tried, have you?

Kasper watches Greg. Just watches him go ...

I didn't hang around, not trying, and get a seat at top table, y'know; I put effort in. And, and now, actually, I have achieved...

This is the first place, actually. Yeah. Y'know? I didn't at home. Right? I wasn't, like, isolated – I had mates – but I did far more schoolwork than the other guys, and that set me apart, so people sometimes... I didn't feel above it, we just didn't... quite sync. Because I was off. But now, here, I have... aligned.

TIMBY Wow. Ahah. Do you think Kasper needs to 'align'? Or 'self-actualise'?

GREG No, not 'self-actualise'. Align. I took the duff parts of myself and binned them. And pinned, to my actual hairy, chest – the robes of a new man. Changed myself.

Painful, but the right thing to do. Because, really, you can and should change to fit your environment when it needs you to. You need new clothes to walk through that door? Get them. Need to speak different? Learn to. Change your brain too, so when you look in the mirror it's all one. Can't really see yourself anymore? That's fine – it's working, and remember: it is for a purpose. Some will say you're conforming, some will take offence, some are so scared they do not move out, and up, do not adapt, get stuck in their patterned armchairs, die through Social Darwinism – and that's fine – that works.

But inside *I* have shifted, *I* have moved to a new type, because *I* could, because *you* can, because *we* can all improve *if we try*.

TIMBY Who's to say this is improvement?

GREG Life. Life does. I didn't know before. You're already behind. From every holiday you don't focus, or get a work placement, you're behind. From school, you're behind. From birth – you, are, behind. These guy's've got it all sewn up, and you are out at sea until you are entirely, entirely in. So you've got to *throw* yourself in, yeah? Do you see? Have to *throw* yourself right in, whatever that entails. That's how I fit in, that's how I caught up, that's how I'm going to win.

TIMBY Feeling pressured to do certain things to fit in is normal – I felt the same coming back – but that cannot involve treating another student in the way you have.

GREG I won't apologise for anything I've done here. Because it *is* what is done here. Why am I the only one being brought in here?

They pause.

TIMBY Maybe we should leave it for now... *(Greg nods)* But I wouldn't be surprised if the Dean wants to follow up with you both.

GREG Whatever she likes.

TIMBY What she likes might be, ahah, suspension, Greg, but...

GREG   Why? We've settled this. Haven't we? Watch us settle this. *(He turns to Kasper and extends his hand.)* Like men. *(Kaspers pauses. Shakes Greg's hand.)* See? No hard feelings.

Timby pauses.

TIMBY   Right then –

Timby and Kasper prepare to finish up.

GREG   Sir, what did you do to fit in? You said you felt the same. Pressured to do certain things. What did you do?

TIMBY   Um... Nothing.

GREG   I've heard there's a true killer of a story. From your first week back here.

TIMBY   Ahah, no, I'm sure –

GREG   Can you tell us?

TIMBY   Sorry?

GREG   The story. People say it's brilliant, Timby – genius.

TIMBY   I am loath to make a fool of myself in a welfare meeting, so...

GREG   Go on.

TIMBY *(pausing)* Kasper doesn't want to hear this, do you? *(Kasper stares at Timby.)* Kasper doesn't want to hear this. Maybe another time. In the pub, or –

GREG   It might help me.

Timby pauses.

TIMBY It is a funny story. *(Little pause)* I presume you mean the night of the dinner for Professor Cantin.

GREG Bang on.

TIMBY Well ... It was my first week back here. I'd been invited to a dinner by my old philosophy tutor, since she was retiring. At the meal I was sat opposite this wonderful person. A lecturer.

GREG What was she like?

TIMBY Yes, incredibly funny. Very involving.

GREG Fit?

TIMBY Beautiful too, I guess. I said grace, and we got to eating and drinking, and talking. We spoke for an age about the university, what it was like to be back. The possibilities of this place seemed never-ending.

(Greg makes a face at Kasper.)

Around us all these games were going on. I think my wine must have been pennied four or five times – you know, where someone –

GREG I know.

TIMBY ... puts a penny in your glass to make you drink it all at once. My mouth was so red it must have looked like the gates of hell. I was becoming looser, that little bit more forward with the lecturer, but it seemed to be going down well. And when they turned to ask a waiter for water, I spied they'd left a full glass.

I stood, and leaned all the way across the table to penny their wine. I put my foot on the chair behind me to launch myself that little bit further – not that normally I'm such an acrobat – but being so drunk I slipped, and fell. With a great crash.

My whole body was splayed across dinner. Guinea fowl, roast potatoes, wine pouring over my back and sides, soaking my suit. I rolled over, onto candelabras and mustard. And when I looked up I saw my professor staring at me in horror. And when I looked behind me I caught the upside-down faces of the students failing to stifle their laughter. I didn't need to look at the lecturer.

I remember it all so clearly because it dawned on me: wow, I have a tainted past, present and future, here. Well done, mate. I tried to laugh myself, but it just made me, sort-of, convulse; shake wine about like some great, labrador.

It created a lot of warm feeling – for that I was thankful – some common ground with the freshers. But these things dress a person in a character. And it can be easy to just fill that character. Even if it's very slowly. Even if you think, at some point, you'll climb out of it, tell people it's all been wrong, the whole time. But it's hard to make excuses for acting a certain way when it's been years. What are those years, if not your character. You see? *(Slight pause.)* The funniest thing. Is that after that night, everyone called me Timby. Which isn't actually even my real –

GREG Not your real name?

TIMBY Well. No my name is –

Greg laughs, turns to Kasper.

GREG Told you it was great, didn't I? Well done Timby, mate – a monster tale. A masterclass in embarrassment. A true pageant of despair.

TIMBY Yes, well. It's a brilliant place, but it's got highs and lows. As with any family.

GREG Can I ask, mate, while we're on you: why did you come back?

TIMBY So many reasons. It's the best place for my PhD. And... it's the best place. Then, you know, even better – this role opens up – paid to help the younger students. It felt right.

GREG Yeah but –

Kasper has a sandwich.

TIMBY Yes, help yourself. You must be hungry.

GREG What'd you do before?

TIMBY Oh, a range of things. Some charity work. Tutoring. Edited an online magazine.

GREG Why'd you stop?

TIMBY I... No I'm not ashamed to say it – these things should be spoken about, especially by me... I had a bit of a, bit of a breakdown, actually.

Kasper and Greg stare. Timby chuckles to himself, has a sandwich.

GREG So... you became a Welfare Officer?

TIMBY Yes. I understand, you see.
  (A pause.) Right. You'll be late for footy.

Greg and Kasper stand to leave.

Kasper glares at Timby – Timby sees – and exits quickly.

Greg is ready with his stuff.

TIMBY Greg, one last thing. I know you're going to ignore much of what I've said, but hear this:

the college, the university, they aren't like the outside world. Outside, everyone's stomping about, shouting their ideas, obsessed with being misunderstood, I think. 'No one gets us', 'no one understands me'. But what do we do here? Study. We take it slow, we explore, we listen. And that way, here, we might understand, and we might be understood.

Timby pauses.

GREG Um, okay.

TIMBY Yes? Good lad. What are you up to this weekend?

GREG We're off to Tall Hugo's place.

TIMBY Very nice.

GREG I'm excited. See ya.

He exits. Timby takes a sandwich, and bins the rest. He takes a bite.

Scene 3

Early afternoon, mid-March.

Greg is by the door, in jeans, shoes, Ralph Lauren polo shirt, jacket, and crown, wearing a satchel and holding a sceptre. Timby stands in cricket whites. Kasper sits small in a chair, wearing chinos, shoes, and an un-tucked and oversized shirt, playing with his signet ring nervously.

TIMBY It's for – It's for – I was playing cricket.

GREG Ah, right, / I see.

TIMBY I didn't have time to –

GREG Yeah no you look great, mate.

TIMBY Greg –

GREG I'm being serious. I'm just shocked. Walked in, thought you'd drafted an umpire – for our 'chat'. *(Slight pause. He gestures to the crown and sceptre.)* Aren't you gonna ask me–?

TIMBY Let's try to keep things...

Slight pause. Indicating Kasper.

GREG Oh what's he said now...?

TIMBY Kasper –

GREG You enjoy this, don't you – bringing us in here – all about you –

TIMBY That's enough, Greg.

Slight pause.

GREG Alright, chill out, Timby. Jeez.

TIMBY You're going to meet with the Dean in thirty minutes.

GREG About –?

TIMBY I asked if I could meet with you first. Because I know you.

Slight pause.

GREG I honestly haven't the foggiest what's... Why would I be meeting the Dean?

TIMBY The incident in the club last Thursday.

GREG Which club?

TIMBY The club you went to last Thursday.

GREG Right but I went to Credit, Sniff, Eternity, Jungle, / Laminate.

TIMBY Jungle? *(Kasper nods)* Jungle.

GREG I don't even remember Jungle, mate.

TIMBY Just listen. It has been reported. By Kasper, and a witness. That in Jungle last Thursday. You forced a kiss on Kasper.

A pause. Then Greg laughs.

TIMBY Greg.

GREG Uh oh – Kas, he's caught us.

TIMBY That's not all.

GREG What else did we get up to? Did I, did I do a bit of–?

TIMBY It is reported. That you forced a kiss. Pushed your tongue into his mouth. Then grabbed his testes.

GREG Grabbed? Grabbed or cupped? Cause a cup is like… A grab is like…

TIMBY Grabbed. His testes. Forcefully.

GREG God I'm kinky when I'm drunk, aren't I?

Slight pause.

TIMBY Are you…? It sounds like you're admitting to having done this?

GREG Sounds like Kas and I are more than just friends now, ey.

TIMBY And you'll tell them this?

GREG 'Them'?

TIMBY The Dean, the Academic Services Manager, Dr Harper, maybe others. They're meeting now – Kasper has just been in to see them – and I am due to –

GREG Yeah, sure, whatever. Tell them. They can use it for one of their senior common room circle jerks – no, the biscuit challenge. Dr Harper aiming for a garibaldi... *(He pauses)* Can I go now? *(Timby hesitates. Goes to speak)* I'll tell 'em anything they like, what does it matter, not like they're gonna kick me out, is it?

A pause. Greg snorts.

GREG Well they're not, are they, so... so... tell 'em whatever they like... *(A pause)* I mean they literally can't, because I haven't actually done anything. *(A pause)* They cannot kick me out over this. I know they can't. So... *(A pause)* Why are you giving me that look? This isn't –

TIMBY Greg, it's simple. College has a pattern. A pattern of assaults – verbal and now physical –

GREG I –

TIMBY ... on Kasper made by you. This is common knowledge amongst students and staff. A number of complaints have been made. An article has been published in a student newspaper –

GREG A what?

TIMBY Kasper has decided not to go to the police, but to allow the college to deal with the allegations internally.

A pause.

GREG They weren't assaults.

TIMBY They think they were.

GREG   I'll say they weren't.

TIMBY   Yes but we think they were. You don't seem to under... stand. *(He pauses)* Punishment by College. Requires that, on balance, they think it more likely you did it than not. *(pause)* You're accountable for your actions, you're old enough now.

GREG   I know. *(He pauses)* Good. Can't wait. Bring it on.

Greg and Timby watch each other.

TIMBY   I'm going in to speak to them now. Wait here. I'll come and collect you. Kasper, I'll see you later.

Greg nods.

Kasper stands, and him and Timby head towards the door. Greg stares straight ahead, thinking.

Timby exits but Kasper stops at the door. He turns and watches Greg.

Greg remembers the crown and sceptre. He takes off the crown, and lays it and the sceptre down, carefully.

He takes his jacket off. Underneath, pinned to his shirt, is a big birthday badge saying '19!' He takes that off too, and puts it down with the crown and sceptre.

He pauses, and thinks.

Kasper closes the door quietly. Greg turns and sees him.

KASPER   We are done with you.
We are done with you.

GREG   I don't...

KASPER   We are blowing you up. *(He stares.)*
You are killing us. You are making us kill ourselves.

Some want 'tolerance'. We know that's not really living. Some value 'living together'. We think it's your world or ours.

We are sick of waiting for progress. There is no such thing as progress.

We have crept past the trenches. We are bringing war to your homes.

We are done with you. We are blowing you up.

GREG   Mate...

KASPER   The word 'mate' will be banned. Phrases like 'the boys', punishable. All caught chanting 'pints pints pints' will have their mouths sewn shut.

We envision you hanging from windows. We foresee harsh medical procedures. We will tolerate mass graves.

You will not be in the universities. You will not run the companies. You will not have your pubs, clubs or bars. You will not even be in the prisons. We do not want to rule you. We want to blow you all up. And have a nicer time. Do you understand?

(Greg stares.) You still think reality is yours... Okay... But it is not now. Not to explain, or describe. Not to define. Not at all. It is ours. And we say it looks like this:

Two boys sit in Hall. Eating. A big blonde one. A hench brunette. Opposite a girl. Their friend. They think of a joke. They do not use her name. Their friend. They call her 'Whore'. Pass the salt, Whore. Out tonight, Whore? Been out Whoring? You big fucking Whore.

What is the joke?

GREG   Yeah, they didn't mean / that.

KASPER She decides that.

GREG No but –

KASPER It's ironic? She decides that. You are hungry for a kebab. You walk to the kebab shop. You see the lights are off. You say 'that's so gay'.

GREG Ahah.

KASPER What is the problem?

GREG Yeah, I get it, it's offensive.

KASPER Yes. Firstly. You implicate a gay man. A gay man has shut your kebab shop. A gay man is a problem here. A gay man should not be a problem here. A gay man is beaten to death in the street.

GREG That's not –

KASPER Yes.

GREG No you're –

KASPER Yes, it means that. Because we say so.

GREG You can't just –

KASPER Your inconvenience no longer justifies our suffering.

Your irony will not work. Your claim to devil's advocate is void. Just because you lack an eyeball-tattoo of a St George's flag does not make you exempt. When you say something, it is ours. And if we want, you mean what you said. And if we want … we melt it down. We forge it into a heavy sword. And we chop your head off.

Unfortunately, in this case, we want. *(He stares.)*

Anyway, enough of that, Gregory. I just want … I want you to understand everything. Really. It's only fair. And know my regret. Sincerely. You see I've been spending a lot of time round you, waiting meekly for you to put the nail in, and it's clear: you are not the worst, by a way. Any of your friends, it could have been them – maybe it should have been them, in an ideal world. But you were the first. And the weakest. And this has to happen quickly. Your kind must be shown early what happens, or the violence goes on, and gets worse. My room is trashed. My genitals crushed in an alley. I hang myself from my ceiling fan. Callum Hardy – a.k.a Shitter – was not queer, but I know his fate could be my own. So no mercy. No compromise. When I get triggered, I pull a trigger. Okay?

GREG Ahah.

KASPER I'll spell it out for you, Gregory. I am now going to destroy you.

College will not side with you. Because there will be protests. I will arrange them. Because this is in one student newspaper already. I will have it in them all. The nationals too.

GREG Yeah, sure, *The Guardian*'s going to –

KASPER Come on. Hate crimes and cover-ups – in this place? Will get them rock-hard.

And you will be hunted. Made a vessel for hate. Your head stuck on a pike on the city wall.

For which I am sorry. *(He pauses. Greg stares.)*

I know what your brain's doing. Not accepting it. Thinking: I'm the rebel. The Loveable Rogue. The Misfit King. I'll get off. We always do, we scoundrels. I'll take my telling off, hit the clubs. Do the shots, mack the birds, ignore the grave I'm digging.

Take my advice. Go quietly. It can get worse.

GREG *(staring)* The fuck are you on about?

KASPER Ahh... you're not listening. I've scared you too much. Let's take a break.

GREG Scare me? Scare me.

KASPER *(pause)* Ahah. 'Lad, lad, lad, lad...'

GREG Well...

KASPER Lad. Lad. Lad. Lad.

GREG Y'know, –

KASPER Lad. Lad. Lad. Lad. Lad. Lad. Lad. Lad. LAD. LAD. LAD. LAD. LAD. LAD. LAD. LAD. LAD, LAD, LAD, LAD. LAD, LAD, LAD, LAD. LAD-LAD-LAD-LAD. LAD-LAD-LAD-LAD. LAD-LAD-LAD-LAD. LADDDDDDDDDDDDDD. LADDDDDDDDDDDDDD. LADDDDDDDDDDDDDD. LADDDDDDDDDDDDDD. LAAAAAAAAA –

Are you feeling comfortable?

GREG I –

KASPER Have you ever noticed... people associate penis size with types of men?

Strong men: big ones. Weak men: little.

What d'you think I have?

You would say: a teeny weeny.

But I have a huge cock, Gregory. Not a diddler, a schlong. Not a pecker, a pole. Terrifyingly large, it is said. Big enough to have gravity, scientists have declared.

Really you should fear it, not me, Gregory. Fear my massive, looming, cock.

But maybe you'd rather that. That it be –

Big or small? Out of interest. If you had to. Take one. Take a cock.

Small? But if you're going to – to take that cock – may as well go for the big one, a real step up from your finger, really work that prostate, give you that mythic orgasm you've always dreamt of.

Isn't small weak? Big strong.

Could you take it? My big fat dick. Could you take my big fat dick? Maybe you'd like it. My big fat dick. Maybe you'd love it. My great groaning big fat –

GREG No I –

KASPER How d'you know? How'd you tell? How'd you –

GREG I'm not.

KASPER Not what?

GREG Not gay.

KASPER Uh oh. Gay panic –

GREG No.

KASPER GAY PANIC. SOUND THE ALARMS, THERE'S A GAY PANIC. DING DING DING DING.

It is always the homophobes.

GREG No –

KASPER No but it's fine to be afraid. To be young, gay and afraid.

GREG No.

KASPER Why'd you kiss me then? Why'd you touch me, the way you did? That wasn't a joke. The passion melted the ice in my glass.

GREG I'd know.

KASPER No, you can't, because you've internalised society's fear. It's formed a hard black shell around your feeling.

Or if not gay, maybe like me – or something like me. Sexuality is a continuum, Gregory – there's some gay in everyone. Every single man fancies at least one other man – in a fully sexual way. Maybe I'm your man.

GREG I'm – normal.

A pause.

KASPER Wrong word. You should see something.

He takes out his phone, sends something. Greg gets a text, checks his phone.

GREG ...no ...

KASPER Yes.

GREG People think we've slept together?

KASPER You lucky boy.

GREG That's insane.

KASPER Insanely hot. Be thankful you got me – there are some ugly queers in this college.

GREG But I –

Kasper is texting.

GREG What are you doing?

KASPER Writing a graphic little tale.

GREG Stop.

KASPER I'm saying you're good.

(Greg darts for the phone; Kasper dodges.)

Oh, this looks excellent for me. Very accomplished. To have caught and turned one of the alphas. Oh boy... *(Greg darts for the phone; Kasper dodges.)* If you lay a hand on me...

GREG No, I...

KASPER Ooh, let's make it a game. *(Greg shakes his head.)* Come on, Gregory, you love your games.

We'll make it physical – we'll flip a coin – I need something easy, you know, being bad at sports. Right –

(He takes a coin from his pocket.) Heads, and I'll text someone from college these sordid details. Tails, and I'll email a paper about you assaulting me.

Ready? *(He flips the coin.)* Heads. Wonderful. I'm going to cycle through my contacts, and you will say stop, and I'll text that person this...

(He sends Greg the text. Greg groans. Greg darts for the phone; Kasper steps back, and holds down the button, watching Greg.) Come on, you coward.

GREG Now.

KASPER Oh no. You've got Willis. He is a real bitch.

GREG Please don't –

Kasper sends the text.

KASPER You must start listening. I know it's tempting to think about a big fart you once did, or a lady with five tits, but if you don't focus, this is going to get nasty. Think: every mistake you make closes some doors. Futures you'll never have. *(He watches Greg. Greg is frozen, looking away.)* Try to imagine, someone you've just met – sparky, involving. Saying your sexuality, part of your being, does not exist. In effect: you don't exist. Can you imagine being denied existence? One at the very least wants to exist. Even the dead exist.

GREG   You're... You're obsessed with me, that's –

KASPER   Oh please. You're not worth it. This is a comma in my diary. I'm hitting the squash courts next.

GREG   Did you write that weird poem? In my pidge? *(beat)* You are obsessed.

KASPER   Ah, bit of fun. I was going through a Romantics phase. And giving you a helpful warning. Not my fault you thought it all about sex. For an English student, you're terrible at subtext.

GREG   This is my life. I'm not some... This isn't a... When Timby finds out –

KASPER   Timby? Timby hates you. He's throwing you to the wolves right now.

GREG   No.

KASPER   He'll come back and ease the blow, but...

GREG   When he knows about you...

KASPER   Knows what? That I'm not jelly? You can tell him my next target, if you like. That might help. A girl named Kara Richards? *(Little pause.)* She's fascinating. What's known as a 'ladette'? Does all the stuff you lads do, but with a fanny.

GREG   Mate...

KASPER   Including using 'gay' pejoratively. She's caught the same disease you have, but it manifests differently in women. It causes this incredible psychosis, where one sides with one's oppressors – and acts like a massive twat.

GREG Not on, mate...

KASPER She actually hangs around with the men who formed the 'I've Slammed Kara Society.' I'd make sure she saw one of the agendas – maybe the meeting where her asshole was discussed in great detail.

GREG You continue we're really gonna fall out...

KASPER I understand why you like her – she's got tits, hasn't she? But she is a total fucking moron, a disgrace, the enemy –

GREG I said watch it.

KASPER *(pausing)* What? That everything? That's you defending your lady? You didn't even touch me.

GREG I'm not... like that.

KASPER What d'you mean? You are that. Are you afraid to hit me? I'm coming for you. I'm coming for it all. Yet still. You aren't even a good lad. You have an inherent weakness not suited to the lifestyle. And that's... *(He pauses.)* I mean I know why, I get it. You won't fight back because deep down, you sense that it is fated. It was always going to happen, because you don't deserve this place.

A pause.

GREG Say that again.

KASPER Not like your friends, not like me. You're not worth it, not good enough. That's why you're tanking it. Boo-hoo-hooing your way to the man at the back of the pub who claims he could have had everything.

GREG Fuck you.

KASPER There he is.

GREG You jealous little fucking, fucking –

KASPER Go for it.

GREG No, shut up. I'm not having it, any of your – This is mine.

Timby enters, suddenly; pauses.

TIMBY Everything alright?

GREG What did she say? The Dean. What did she say?

TIMBY I don't think I should –

GREG Tell me.

Timby pauses. Glances at Kasper.

TIMBY Shall we sit, boys?

GREG Tell me.

TIMBY Let's sit. Are you okay, Kas?

Kasper looks down and away, tears in his eyes.

GREG He's fine.

TIMBY Greg...

GREG For God's sake, he's fine. Tell him you're fine. He isn't afraid, he's making this up.

TIMBY Stop, Greg, please.

Greg grabs Kasper.

GREG Speak. Speak.

TIMBY Let go of him, Greg.

Timby tries to separate them. Greg pushes him off.

GREG Say something. Speak. Speak. SPEAK.

Timby tries to separate them. Greg pushes him off –

Timby stumbles and knocks himself.

Greg and Kasper pause and watch Timby. Timby stands, shocked.

TIMBY I'll –

He exits, quickly.

Kasper and Greg look at each other.

KASPER Thank you.

Kasper plants a tiny kiss on Greg.

Greg attacks Kasper.

They scuffle.

They separate.

Kasper lets out a sigh of relief.

Interlude

Night. A dark room in the living room-kitchen of a small house in Spain in the late 1930s.

A military cot in the middle of the room. A young doctor, resembling Kasper, sitting up in bed, just woken. There is a dim lamp beside him.

In the doorway, in darkness, The General. The General resembles Timby.

THE GENERAL Nightmare.

DOCTOR What?

THE GENERAL Nightmare.

DOCTOR *(pausing)* Would you like something, General Franco? Something to help you sleep?

The General comes into the room. He is in pyjamas.

DOCTOR I can, I can –

The General climbs into bottom of the bed.

THE GENERAL Warm.

He slides his feet up the bed. The doctor jumps. The General stares.

DOCTOR Cold feet.

THE GENERAL Crumpets.

DOCTOR Sorry?

THE GENERAL Do you have any?

DOCTOR I ... *(He sees some on the side.)* I do. Would you like some, General?

The General nods. The doctor gets out of bed and starts to toast the crumpets.

THE GENERAL I don't know if you notice, but I eat a lot of crumpets.

A slight pause.

DOCTOR No?

THE GENERAL In the morning, Doctor. Dozens. So many. The quantity has actually brought comment from some. The sheer volume of crumpets I guzzle before I get to work. They ask: why does he do it? How does he do it? It makes him so greasy, like a seal. Fatter – also like a seal. It is so particular. So why do I do it, Doctor?

They pause.

DOCTOR You like crumpets, General.

THE GENERAL Exactly.

The doctor brings the General the crumpets. The General takes them, and starts eating.

DOCTOR General Franco ...

THE GENERAL Get back into bed, Doctor. Warmer. *(The doctor does so. The General eats.)* My father was in the military, –

DOCTOR I thought –

THE GENERAL Let's say he was. He always told me: your heart is a muscle too. By which I took him to mean: beneath sentiment, physical reality remains. What do you think of that?

DOCTOR Wise words for the head of an army, General.

THE GENERAL Exactly. Smart boy. What is your favourite part of the body, Doctor?

The doctor pauses.

DOCTOR The shoulders, General.

THE GENERAL I've never heard the shoulders.

DOCTOR I like the shape.

The General touches the doctor's shoulders.

THE GENERAL The shoulders... Yes, okay. The frame. The architecture. Yes. Mine is the thighbone. What's that called?

DOCTOR The femur.

The General touches the doctor's inner thigh, under the covers.

THE GENERAL The femur is excellent. It'll take an incredible amount of pressure. Especially for something so close to something so soft. *(He pauses.)* How excellent is it I can do this and it not mean anything? I can climb into your bed. Touch you. There. But it doesn't mean anything I don't want it to. Were another man to do that, he'd be called a deviant. If I found out, I'd judge him guilty and have him killed. Is that hypocritical? No. It's not anything. Did I just touch you? Yes. Now I say I didn't – no. Isn't that fantastic?

DOCTOR ...depends ...

THE GENERAL Excuse me?

DOCTOR That depends, General.

THE GENERAL Yes. It does. You are a smart boy.

A pause.

DOCTOR General Franco...

THE GENERAL My sleep is off. Short nights, the shelling – makes my dreams abnormal.

DOCTOR I could give you / something –

THE GENERAL My mother... She'd do shadow puppets. Father at war. Father fighting wolves. Father in the vampire's castle. She was very good. Contortable, adaptable little hands. But her true trick was to take my nightmares and show me them, and, and turn them into tales of hope. Father stands triumphant over the fallen. Father bests the wolf. Father escapes the vampire's castle. After watching the shadow-plays from the safety of bed I would sleep soundly.

Oh, to have the clarity of a black shadow on a white wall. Now my mind is so full – my nightmares roil and tumble. Statues and folk songs. Mussolini and Hitler. All the possible fates of the country. But I have no one to do shadow-plays for me. So I sort of make my own. *(beat)* Would you like to hear tonight's nightmare? *(The doctor pauses.)* Would you like to hear my nightmare, Doctor? *(The doctor nods.)*

I was watching two boys and a man. In an old building. The clothing and talk were futuristic, but the types were old. The flabby intellectual. The ambitious young buck. The quiet deviant. The ditherer looked like me. The spirited boy like my protégé. The abnormal one like you. *(beat)* They spoke of me, actually. As long dead. Flippantly. I waited for them to speak of me again, but it moved onto less important matters. All regarding the deviant. Protecting the deviant, rewarding the deviant. I thought: what kind of future is this? I woke myself up. Now those men are gone. *(He gets out of bed.)*

That was lovely, thank you. Good to get a bit snuggly. Especially in a war. Gotta make time for the snuggles, in a war. *(He picks up the lamp, Starts to move towards some curtains before a window, stops.)* Did you dream? *(The doctor goes to speak –)*

Tell me.

DOCTOR I was in a kind of waiting room. It was suddenly my turn. I went to the door, opened it. Beyond was this room. The light was thick like jelly. I could feel the stars were close, outside. You were standing where you are now. Then you moved to draw the curtains. But so slow. Everything had slowed down. I felt for the first time that I could really see things. How they moved. There was this whispering –

THE GENERAL Whispering?

DOCTOR Over everything. You could hear them but you were blocking them out. Myriad voices. I watched myself trying to be strong. Planning how to keep dignity when the time came. Then you woke me up.

Slight pause.

THE GENERAL I don't like that.

DOCTOR Are you going to draw the curtains?

The General pauses.

THE GENERAL Nightmare or dream, I take heart in the inevitability of morning. Waking when I was a boy, it would be dark. Mother would come in. Turn the lamp bright.

(He turns the lamp up to full.) Go to the curtains. *(He goes to the curtains.)* Show me how the night ran out. *(He draws the curtains. Behind them is a soldier who looks just like Greg.)*

He's a mute. Had his mouth sewn shut as a boy, for prattling too much.

The General turns to the soldier, and nods towards the doctor.

The soldier draws a knife and starts towards the doctor. The doctor watches him, chin up –

Then starts out of this and rambles, stumbling out of bed, backing away.

DOCTOR No, no – I know what you're – I am not a deviant. I hate deviants – it was a mistake – I have a young wife – the man made a mistake – I was checking a sore on his thigh and he thought I was –

As the soldier reaches the doctor and swings back the knife, time slows down. The light thickens. Myriad voices whisper.

All three men close their eyes.

As the knife hits the doctor's heart –

Lights down.

ACT TWO

Scene 1

Timby's study. Late afternoon, mid-June.

Bright sunlight outside. The air in the room is hot, close. In the distance, the sounds of a protest.

Kasper is alone, on his mobile, pacing. He is in a white shirt – top button undone – black trousers, shoes, and a formal examination gown. There's a rucksack propped nearby. He looks like he hasn't slept well in weeks.

KASPER I'm sleeping fine. Yes I am. You can't tell over the phone.

Mother, look... I know you are, but –

I have it in hand.

Why should I? If I want to speak to them about it, why do I have to ask you? I know what I'm doing. Being in the paper, for this cause, is only a good thing. It's important.

You can't help. Well – Just, stay out of it. If they contact you: tell me, don't say a thing.

It'll quiet down after today, anyway. I'll get a break. I'm looking forward to coming –

(He stiffens.) Yes, I am very sure.

I do not. I take things just far enough.

He's a bully. He gets what he deserves.

You sound like – You know I'm not the villain here, right? Why do – Why should I feel like the villain? With what he's done. Just because I ... Okay so what do you mean, then?

It looks good for me. I'm taking a stand, won't that –

I'll take that risk. That's a price I'll pay – I'll happily get hurt. Yes I will.

Why are you saying this now? It's literally –

I'm putting the phone down. Yes I am. Say goodbye. I'm putting the –

I am in the right. I will not back down; so say –

Do not make me hang up on you. I will. I will if you don't stop –

(He puts the phone down.)

GOOD CHRIST ALIVE ...

He takes a moment, calms himself.

He gets out a cigarette and opens a window – the sound of the protest and the scrum grow louder.

He smokes by the window, watching the people outside. Rubs his eyes, shakes off the tiredness.

A door opening out in the hall, nearby. Kasper notices. The door closing.

Kasper goes to chuck his cigarette out the window, stops, has a few deep tokes.

The sound of someone just outside. Kasper chucks the cigarette out the window. The door opens – Kasper hasn't breathed out. Timby enters in his usual outfit, plus an examination gown. He sees Kasper.

TIMBY Kas. Didn't realise you were stopping –

(He pauses and sniffs the air.)

Could you close that please? People tend to smoke outside and it gets in here, it gets in my bedroom …

(Kasper partially closes the window. Timby brings over a framed photograph he's carrying.)

Just bought this at the print shop off the high street. Local woman. Think she's captured the quad nicely. The age of it, the bricks. Somehow the light has that, almost physical quality. What d'you think?

(Kasper nods appreciatively. As he goes to put the photo on a shelf, looking at Kasper:)

How were your exams? *(Kasper shrugs – 'okay'.)*

Hot, I'll bet. *(Kasper nods, pantomimes: 'too hot'.)*

I've been invigilating some third year philosophers. The room was… just awful.

(Kasper needs to breathe out. He points at the photo.)

What? Is it … You think it needs … left a bit?

As Timby stares at the photo, Kasper breathes smoke out the window and shuts it. Timby turns.

KASPER Ignore me, ignore me – looks great. How are you?

Kasper keeps an eye on what's going on outside as they talk.

TIMBY Oh! Yes. Okay. A difficult day, of course. Having to wade through that scrum of ... angry young warriors, shall we say, didn't make it any more pleasant. A placard caught me on the – You know I support one's right to protest, but...

KASPER Sally was telling me it's been causing some... debates.

TIMBY Yes. The last Welfare and Equality Committee meet was... heated. Then I met with the Dean and the Master – I swear they almost had a duel. Anyway...

KASPER Cricket was fun yesterday?

TIMBY Very. We lost, but. The drinks after were...

KASPER Oh yeah?

TIMBY I thought cricketers would be a bit more civilized. Then I find myself perched on the roof of a canal boat at two in the morning, using my bat for balance. I really shouldn't have. Long day. And I've got a date later.

KASPER Ooh. Who with?

TIMBY The lecturer.

KASPER The lecturer? The one you covered in guinea fowl?

TIMBY Ahah. Yes. That came up. I addressed it. And... We're doing early dinner at a French bistro, then an organ recital.

KASPER Get the blood going, ey.

(There's a loud 'booooooo' from outside; Kasper looks out.) Well, it's great to hear you'll be getting a good fucking tonight, Timby. *(They both freeze. Kasper*

turns to Timby.) I mean – Ahah. Nothing like a good fucking, ey? I had a great fucking the other night. Fucking, being fucked, it's –

TIMBY I don't think –

They both pause.

KASPER You know I have no idea what I just said.

TIMBY You're under a lot of pressure.
(Slight pause.) You look tired.

KASPER No, no. Well, you know. A lot on my mind. It's sort of taken over everything. Even my dreams.

TIMBY I saw you in the paper.

KASPER Yeah, they were pretty insistent, you know. Someone gave them my name, and I... thought it was best to say my piece.

TIMBY Mm. It didn't sound like you.

KASPER No? Really?

TIMBY You came off very angry.

KASPER They tend to do that. Right? The papers.
(Slight pause.) But no I am angry. I've always been angry. I'm just struggling to cover it when I'm being –

TIMBY Of course. It's understandable. The investigation, the hearings, they've really dragged on. But, College is going to sort it out. Have faith. We don't need to be... looking outside.

One of the porters was telling me they've had journalists pretending to be tourists, sneaking around Halls. It's disgraceful. That plus the protests – We're trying to do exams. God knows how they all found out the final appeal was happening today.

KASPER Probably the journalists ...

TIMBY Yes. So I think, yes, let's stay away from –

KASPER Sure, sure; anyway it'll be over soon. *(A little pause. Kasper watches Timby carefully.)* Greg will be gone, and we can forget this ever happened.

(Timby goes to his desk.) Greg *will* be gone, won't he?

TIMBY I can't say. He has his Master's Appeal, so...

Timby takes his fancy chocolate out of his drawer.

KASPER But the hearings found him guilty. Decided to send him down. *(Timby gestures to Kasper: 'want some?')* This final appeal is a formality. No thanks.

Timby goes to some electronic scales on a shelf.

TIMBY Well, it is and it isn't. It's up to the Master, and if the Master decides to be lenient...

KASPER But why would he? When a whole panel has –

TIMBY It's up to him.

Timby is weighing his chocolate.

KASPER Have you seen the Master recently?

TIMBY Yes.

KASPER Which way is he leaning?

TIMBY I really can't say. Sorry. *(He starts to eat his chocolate.)*

KASPER Maybe I should go and speak to him.

TIMBY He's read your testimony – he emailed me earlier. He's meeting with Greg in the next half hour.

Kasper pauses.

KASPER I'm due to be going out soon – to celebrate finishing exams. I need to get changed. You mind if I...?

TIMBY Mind if you?

KASPER Just change in here. I'll just –

TIMBY ...not a changing room ...

KASPER Sorry?

TIMBY Go ahead. Go for it, very good.

He turns around. Kasper slowly begins to get changed into a sharp new outfit.

KASPER I'm surprised you aren't angry.

TIMBY Hm?

KASPER At Greg.

TIMBY Oh, I am, I am.

KASPER No but I can't remember when I wasn't last angry. Maybe I've always been – No, there must have been a time when I wasn't. But ... I think it started at school. The anger. It was settled in my mind then that any kind of queerness was a no-go. My contact with it was so limited. I dreaded it. Boy did I dread it. So I used the word 'gay' against others just like everybody else. But when I did that, it made me angry – I think in part because I knew it was wrong – speaking like that. But probably also, of course, because I had some sense I wasn't straight ...

That dread of being gay did not let up. I dreaded it so much, I started to think – 'what happens if I'm gay?' I was, I was certain, attracted to women, but the fear of being gay became so present, that I honestly couldn't tell what I was. And by this point, people, culture, had started to tell me I could be gay, but the desire not to be was so deeply ingrained – I'd think, 'you can be, but you aren't, are you? It'd be easier not to be. Safer not to be'. I started to wonder if some part of me wanted to be gay – if part of me wanted drama, or to be provocative, or just to be a more interesting person – like maybe I wanted to be Oscar Wilde, or Auden.

I kept going round, and round – this spiral of dread and desire. I knew this spiral would eventually break me. And I'd kill myself. Which made me so angry – and that anger made me confront myself. I finally just looked at myself. Recognised what I am. I'm bi.

Out of that violence, came something. Something that was mine.'

Timby is tidying his shelves.

TIMBY   Sorry, just to – Are you done changing yet?

KASPER   Sure.

Timby turns – Kasper's shirtless.

TIMBY   Um, I –

KASPER   This was just before coming here. I was excited. The place has associations with sexual freedom, right. Lying in the long grass or floating down the river, chinos a size too small.

TIMBY   Ahah.

KASPER But I hadn't figured out yet how to be public. How to be myself, publicly. And, of course, pretty quickly, the wrong people began to ask. I wanted to deny it. Which made me so furious I couldn't any longer – so I was public. But being public gave them more power. Suddenly they could take part in my sexuality. Chunks of me were carved off, and given out, for any random purpose. I had to be so strong – couldn't duck anything – any small comment, slight knock – in the moment – attack attack attack. *(He pauses.)*

I've found a small community. The club nights aren't much better than school discos. There are odd fault lines – like those who dress like Madonna versus those who dress like they're in Brideshead. Some don't trust me because I'm bi. But there's at least something. For the first time. Now, many of them are angry at me for causing all this. I need to move on.

Kasper pauses, fully dressed. He looks very sharp.

TIMBY New clothes?

KASPER Mm.

TIMBY A jazzy... number.

KASPER You have to be sure of yourself to wear something like this.

Slight pause.

TIMBY I'm sorry this has happened. I, I, I should've –

KASPER Timby. What is going on?

TIMBY The Master's instinct is to be lenient. He knows Greg must be punished. But I think he likes Greg. That's not the only – There are other circumstances to consider.

KASPER Like what?

Timby pauses.

TIMBY Greg's father has been unwell. His mother phoned college especially to –

KASPER So what? I mean that's awful for him – his poor family – but how is that relevant?

TIMBY I guess the question. As the Master sees it. Is whether this is abnormal behaviour for Greg. So, whether he might turn himself around. If he is sufficiently punished. A suggestion has been that he lose his scholarship –

KASPER Your suggestion?

TIMBY ...which in his circum – Sorry? I – Well. I think it would be hard on him. How would you feel about that?

KASPER Betrayed. Because... while it's an interesting proposal. Is it sufficient? Is it not him, here, that is the problem? Must not that link – between him and here – be severed? Do we not need time to heal? And perhaps, as a community, as an institution, to change?

TIMBY Ah, yes, well. Another suggestion. Was some time off. A suspension, for all of next year. Which could, I think, give us time, and Greg time, to –

KASPER It only works if he goes.

Timby pauses.

TIMBY Interesting you say 'work'. 'Work, working.' What we want, see, is for it to work. If Greg goes, it has not worked. This. Me. We have failed him.

KASPER You want to fail me / instead.

TIMBY No, we must still try to help. Understand. Hard as it / may be.

KASPER It's wrong – he deserves / to go.

TIMBY 'Deserve', ahah – I'm never ... sure about / that word.

KASPER It's justice.

TIMBY Ooh, wow, for is it not maybe the pressure? Has he not only made mistakes? What if he's mixed up, trying to understand you – what if your relationship –

KASPER Relationship?

TIMBY I mean – I don't mean – I mean –

Timby pauses.

KASPER Have you heard rumours?

TIMBY I've seen messages. *(He pauses.)* Which make it look. To some. Like this is a... 'lover's quarrel'.

KASPER Would you mind?

TIMBY Sorry?

KASPER You think I've lied to you?

TIMBY No. It's that –

KASPER It would excuse assault and –?

TIMBY No. It's just. Whether these are. Um. Signs Greg should be helped. *(Kasper stares.)* Those messages you sent.

KASPER Jokes.

TIMBY Jokes?

KASPER I have a dark sense of humour. *(beat)* So you think Greg should stay?

TIMBY I didn't...

KASPER You do or you don't?

TIMBY I...

KASPER You could be a force for good.

Slight pause.

TIMBY Oh, thank you.

Kasper moves closer to Timby.

KASPER If you didn't try to appeal to them.

TIMBY Who?

KASPER The Gregs. You feel beholden to them. Which is hard to escape. But I've seen when you cast that off – you're suddenly electric. *(Kasper puts his hand on Timby's arm.)* You get the chance to pass judgement, here. Tell them what you think is right – it will happen. Do you think Greg should stay?

Timby pauses.

TIMBY No.

KASPER Then email the Master again and tell him. *(Timby hesitates. Then takes out his phone, and begins to write an email. Kasper watches him write it.)* That's a bit – I mean – Greg was violent towards you. He scares us. They're going to let him off. I think you can be a bit more ...

(Timby hesitates. Writes another line.) That should do it. *(Timby hesitates. Clicks send. Kasper walks over to a chair by the record player, sits, and sighs. Timby is staring at his phone.)*

Phew. Now we can relax, ey?

(Timby is still staring at his phone. Kasper looks at what's on the deck of the record player. He switches it on, and puts the needle down. 'Waterloo Sunset' by The Kinks begins. Timby looks up.) Wonderful.

(Kasper nods along. Then sings. Then dances a little. Kasper sees Timby watching him. Stops the song. Kasper picks up his stuff, and goes over to Timby.) Thank you, Timby. You're one of the good ones.

He holds out his hand. Timby shakes it, absently.

Kasper exits, closing the door behind him.

Timby is still. Then he checks his cuffs, distracted.

He paces to his desk, and back, and to his desk.

He inefficiently tries to fling something from it in anger.

A door opening out in the hall, nearby. Timby hears. Then the door closing. Timby readies himself.

A knock at the study door.

TIMBY Yes?

GREG It's, uh, Greg? Can I come in?

Timby hesitates.

TIMBY No, yes of course. *(Greg opens the door. He's in a smart shirt, tie, trousers, shoes, plus a formal gown. He has been hit by eggs.)* Shit. I mean –

GREG Yeah. A few of the protestors, outside college, had...

TIMBY Do you want–? I have some spare clothes, I think, you could –

GREG That's okay. Do you have a plastic bag? *(Timby removes his lunchbox from a plastic bag, and hands the bag to Greg.)* Cheers. *(He puts the plastic bag down on a chair, and sits on it with a slow crunch.)*

TIMBY Squash and biscuits.

He starts to get them ready.

GREG The Master's going to chuck me, isn't he?

TIMBY Perhaps he will be lenient.

GREG How, after all this? They need to make a statement.

TIMBY No. The Master isn't like that. He knows you're bright. He knows your background. He's been informed of your current circumstances.

GREG None of them care.

Timby lays out the squash and biscuits.

TIMBY Help yourself. *(Greg stares.)* What are you going to say to him?

GREG Deny it all.

TIMBY You're past that.

GREG Tell him what Kasper's really like.

Timby pauses. Then goes to his desk and starts to cut up the address section of old envelopes.

TIMBY Anyway...

GREG He's –

TIMBY What do you expect? You attacked him.

GREG It wasn't – He made me.

TIMBY That's not an excuse.

GREG He wants to destroy me.

TIMBY He could've gone to the police, Greg. You could be facing assault charges.

GREG He went to the press –

TIMBY No. They found out, they came to / him.

GREG He arranged the protests. He's punishing you, too. Because you tried to help me. It's an obsession. It was a trap. He told me, Timby – he did a speech.

TIMBY A speech?

GREG A whole speech.

TIMBY Not a speech, surely.

GREG A speech, seriously. How would you define a speech?

TIMBY A speech? I don't know – Ten sentences? For a proper speech?

GREG A proper speech – easily ten sentences.

TIMBY That does sound like a speech, but –

GREG He did a speech. He thinks I represent something. That I'm a, a symbol of something. What he's making me. And you're all going along with it. You're meant to protect me. I thought you saw me. And I'm here, screaming at you, 'this is me', and you're saying I'm this. As if I'm a – Not me standing right here. He's a manipulative little –

TIMBY   See, Greg, you can't help yourself! You have done things.

GREG   Not those –

TIMBY   ...and said things.

GREG   He's – *(He pauses)* It's all over...

TIMBY   No – I mean...

GREG   Exam this morning was dog-shit. Can't concentrate. Keep having to leave the library for people looking at me. Not sleeping, anyway. Meant to start English exams next week.

TIMBY   I'm sure they'll – if you don't – let you / resit.

GREG   Mates've fucked off slowly but surely. Very efficient, actually. I'm just not there. You know, they were a part of this too, but now they can't seem to remember any of it. 'I do not recall to that'. Fair enough, save yourself – but apparently I'm too much hassle now. They're off with schoolmates, or in London. Life. I miss Life. Life is absolutely fucked for me, now.

TIMBY   Oh, no...

GREG   No one tells me when they're going. I miss the hot dogs.

TIMBY   I'm sorry, what are you –?

GREG   Life. Just off the high street.

TIMBY   It's a club...

GREG   Yeah! Ahah.

TIMBY   Hot dogs?

GREG Right by the dance floor. Those watery ones.

Little pause.

TIMBY Maybe some time off –

GREG I went home last weekend. My schoolmates were weird. There was no... spark. Couple of them mocked my accent. Said I'm starting to sound like a 'chinless wonder'.

TIMBY That's not / nice.

GREG And my parents. Are getting actual calls from actual papers. Like... ones Dad's reading, in his armchair; he literally gets a call from the paper he's looking at. In what universe? Hour after hour, and he really needs... the rest... They've pinned all their hopes on me. When I got in, their expectations... woosh. Now... I can see it draining them. Timby, I feel so ill. Like, pure nerves. Expectation.

TIMBY Sounds like a panic attack.

GREG It's like when you're about to cum, –

TIMBY Oh – well, maybe / it's –

GREG But all the time. It's like I'm permanently about to cum.

TIMBY Sounds... stressful.

GREG It's like when your mum walks in, –

TIMBY I don't...

GREG ... when you're just about to blow, –

TIMBY Oh, really, I don't –

GREG ... and everything slows down. And you yell 'Nooooooooo, Mummmmm'. But you sort of want to. Cum. You know?

TIMBY I. No.

GREG And after, after your mum has seen you do that, and you're hunched over, sticky-palmed, you think: I should've locked my door. That's the reasonable thing. No shame. No trauma for Mum. But I'm a daredevil, you know. I'm scared, Timby.

TIMBY I know.

GREG Keep imagining sitting in the waiting room for job interviews. Staring at the door. Wondering if they've looked me up... I don't know what I'll do. I really need this.

Timby goes and sits beside Greg. Pats his shoulder.

You know, with all this, I've actually got a spare ticket to Captain's Cocktails tonight.

TIMBY Oh, really?

GREG Maybe we could go. If I'm not packing. You might be my last mate here.

TIMBY Perhaps.

GREG Yeah? Awesome. Hey, will you come in with me? To see the Master. I'd feel better about it.

Timby pauses.

Maybe you could say something.

Timby pauses.

Timby mate, do you really think I should be sent down? Ruined?

TIMBY That's not –

GREG What it amounts to. Do you?

TIMBY In these circumstances, some action must be taken.

GREG But this?

Timby pauses.

TIMBY No.

GREG Then come tell him that.

TIMBY I've already told him –

GREG This?

TIMBY No.

GREG You might make the difference. You have to do what you know is right. Timby –

He puts his hand on Timby's knee – Timby moves away.

TIMBY Is there anything you haven't told me? I can't just – I'd need new –

GREG Kasper's speech?

TIMBY A speech is not a reason. But if you were... – There was a rumour you and Kasper might've... been... *(Greg stares.)* Which would not excuse what you've done. But might change. In the Master's eyes. The tenor. Of your actions. What you've said. If you were...

GREG As in am I...? *(He pauses)* Course I'm not. Not me.

Timby pauses.

TIMBY It's time to accept you may have to move on. I know these things feel all important, but they aren't. I promise.

GREG *(looking at the floor)* ...you have to...

TIMBY Greg, I've –

GREG No you have to. Or I'll... report you...

TIMBY What did you say?

GREG Just come in there. Stop this.

TIMBY Greg what do you mean you'll –?

GREG I'll tell them you've been inappropriate. With us. Students you're meant to be helping.

TIMBY Ridiculous.

GREG Is it? You force us to talk about personal stuff, when it's clear we don't want to. You made me read that poem. You looked at me while I changed.

TIMBY No I –

GREG You make me uncomfortable. Others, too. These meetings are... off. I'll tell them I've felt like you want me to... That you've tried to make me... –

Kasper starts to enter, unseen.

TIMBY Get out.

GREG Timby...

TIMBY Never. I'd never. Get out.

GREG TIMBY. YOU HAVE TO. Don't make me.

They notice Kasper.

TIMBY Kasper, Greg and I have a few things to –

KASPER I think I should be here, actually.

TIMBY That's – I mean – / No.

KASPER What was that? Just now?

Greg and Timby pause.

GREG I'm going to report Timby. For being inappropriate.

TIMBY What does that mean?!

Kasper stares.

KASPER Go on, then.

TIMBY What?

KASPER I've got this.

GREG I will.

KASPER Okay.

TIMBY No. Why would you–?

KASPER Door's right there.

Greg pauses.

GREG Look, Kas.

KASPER You see?

GREG This has gone too far. Let's sort it some other way. Like what d'you want?

KASPER Feels obvious at this point.

GREG What else? Like you can have a free punch.

KASPER Anywhere?

GREG Anywhere.

KASPER Oh my.

Greg presents himself.

GREG However many you like, I'll stand here.

TIMBY   This is an office.

KASPER   That is exciting. But no.

GREG   You're not being reasonable, mate.

KASPER   I am being so fucking reasonable, I'm getting nosebleeds.

GREG   Look. I hear you. I swear. But all this? I'm losing friends.

KASPER   So am I.

GREG   I'm getting death threats.

KASPER   Me too.

GREG   People are going after my parents.

(Kasper pauses.)

Please. Alright? Kas? Please. I'm sorry. I don't even know why I... It's not been me.

KASPER   You feel you've made mistakes.

GREG   Yes.

KASPER   But so many. Over and over. They aren't mistakes. They're just you.

GREG   No...

KASPER   This isn't you. This is just depressing. Come on. Boots on, chin up, and leave the trench. Get it over with. But live it! You're good at that. A blaze of glory, a –

TIMBY   Stop it, Kasper. I know you're upset, but – *(Kasper goes to reply)* – No. Just stop.

KASPER   He's humiliated you.

TIMBY   No, he...

KASPER I'm ending that. You just can't handle it.

TIMBY Well... Yes. But that's fine. That's just alright with me.

KASPER It's hard. Because it matters. Move past your pity.

GREG Timby...

KASPER There's nothing more to be done, Gregory – yes? Nothing to be –

TIMBY Hey. Enough of that. This isn't the playground. We don't decide things this way.

KASPER Wake up. These situations are always decided like this – it's just usually the other way round. Most don't make as big a fuss as him – but the damage is there. The violence spirals on. After people like you look away. Yeah – you. Violence follows people like you. You could have prevented this, Timby. You're the Welfare Officer. I was not faring well. You saw the cause. College saw the cause. But you just wanted it to go away. Quickly quickly, –

TIMBY No...

KASPER ... under the rug – no matter the consequences. So I had to act.

TIMBY That's... Look. There are fairer ways than –

KASPER You were the fairer way.

TIMBY I... Listen. I mean, what exactly will this achieve? This, it's only – you're hurting one boy.

KASPER Crush that one boy, show the others, maybe they won't do it again. Catch it here, maybe we can stop it spreading.

TIMBY   Ahah. That's...

KASPER *(stares)* When they see how I have destroyed him, Timby. They will fear me.

TIMBY *(pauses)* 'Fear you?' What are you saying, Kas? You don't want people to fear you.

KASPER   If I have to, I have to.

TIMBY   You don't need to be feared –

KASPER   We do. Even if it's horrible. Because this will keep happening. It's getting worse, turning back – you know it.

Timby pauses.

KASPER   We can't keep... They come for our throats. We make placards.

TIMBY   I know.

KASPER   They bury us. We kiss their clenched fists. I just want not to lose. Once.

TIMBY   I understand. But you still don't get to decide this boy's fate. I'm sorry. *(He pauses)* Maybe no one has to lose. Let's all go see the Master, we can talk about what's happened here. Put it all out there. Figure out a way through / together.

KASPER   No...

TIMBY   Kas. Your way. Which is not fair. Might make it worse, yes? You've, you've, cast into doubt everything you've –

KASPER   I don't care anymore. I can't.
(Greg and Timby watch Kasper.)
Doesn't matter if you think I'm wrong.

TIMBY I... don't, Kas. But I still care. So I'm going in to see / the Master with Greg.

GREG Thank you.

TIMBY You can come tell your side if you want.

KASPER If you stand in my way... I might think he has a point. Regarding your behaviour. That is what I'll discuss with the Master.

A pause.

TIMBY Really, Kas?
(Timby and Kasper watch each other.)
Really?

Kasper looks away.

KASPER Timby... If you go in now, he'll doubt the whole thing.

GREG Timby, no, look at me.

KASPER But you know it's true –

GREG Do I deserve this?

KASPER ... even if I've...

Timby pauses, watching them.

TIMBY I am so very sorry. Both of you.

He looks at his watch. Hesitates. Looks to Kasper.

TIMBY If I... No more of this.

GREG Timby...

TIMBY You leave him be.

/ Kasper pauses.

GREG Please, Timby, no...

Kasper nods. Timby turns to Greg.

TIMBY It's time, Greg.

Greg pauses. And goes slowly to his knees.

GREG Please.

TIMBY You need to go.

KASPER I'm sorry.

GREG Please.

TIMBY You need to go.

KASPER I'm sorry.

GREG Please.

They pause. Then Greg stands, and removes his gown. Folds it up, and lays it on the seat with the plastic bag. Leaves the room. Silence.

KASPER This is what it's going to take.

(Timby doesn't reply.) We had to.

(Timby won't look at him.) Timby…

You'll see.

Kasper leaves. Timby closes the door.

The phone on his desk rings. He ignores it. The ringing stops, and a message begins to play:

BELINDA *(voice)* Hello love, it's Belinda calling. I've just had a tute with Kara Richards and Sally Jotson, and suggested they come see you. They've had a falling out and, well, I'm keen we get it sorted out before it develops further. They'll be on their way now, if you can. Hope that's okay. Hope you're okay. See you soon.

He remains still. Then realises what the message said. He goes to the window and looks out. Sees the women coming. He looks about his room. He rearranges the squash and biscuits. He bags up Greg's gown, and goes to stuff it away. He catches himself in the mirror. Studies his face. He tries smiling.

TIMBY   Sally... Kara... hello... how're... *(He shakes his head. Tries smiling again.)* College is... community... family. *(He shakes his head. Tries smiling again.)* External... all a bit... time of year. Come on...

(He repositions himself. Tries smiling again.) Listen to... understand... woman-to – Come on, come on...

(He shakes his arms out, and his head. Tries smiling again.) Versed in... side of the... here to... Timby you – Ah.

(He slaps his face. Tries smiling again.) Whatever it... get you... I can – No no no...

(He clenches his fists, bares his teeth at the mirror and whines. Out in the hallway, a door opening, then closing.) Help, help, help, help.

A knock at the door. He pauses. He puts his hands over his face and crushes himself up as small as possible. Bursts out and stares hard at the mirror. Smiles the right smile.

TIMBY   Come in.

The door handle turns.

Lights down.

The End.